The Chester Mystery Cycle

The Chester Mystery Cycle
A New Staging Text

by
EDWARD BURNS

Department of English Language and Literature,
University of Liverpool

Liverpool University Press

First published 1987 by

LIVERPOOL UNIVERSITY PRESS
PO BOX 147
LIVERPOOL
L69 3BX

British Library Cataloguing in Publication Data
Data is available

ISBN 0-85323-046-3

Word-processed in the
Department of English Language and Literature, University of Liverpool

Printed and bound by
Eaton Press Limited, Wallasey, Merseyside

The Chester Mystery Cycle
A New Staging Text

Part Three: The Redemption of Mankind

Introduction

The text of the Chester plays as presented here is a modern acting version, prepared for performance at Chester Cathedral from 30 June to 12 July 1987, under the direction of Bob Cheeseman. The text is as it went into rehearsal on 1st May.

As an introduction to the text, I have provided some notes, first on the history and nature of the cycle, then on my work in 'translating' it, then on some aspects of its staging requirements.

Evidence and Context

Anyone who visits a great medieval cathedral will have some idea of the life that went on around it, of the pageantry, ritual and entertainment that linked it to medieval city life. Central to this picture is the 'Mystery' play - a series of biblical episodes performed as a kind of festival by amateur actors connected to the 'guilds', the organizations of craftsmen and merchants who controlled entry to their profession, and its trading policies. 'Mystery' in this context means 'specialized skill' of this kind, not religious mysticism. But precise knowledge of the cycles - how they were performed, when, by and for whom - is hard to get hold of, and a kind of myth has grown up around them, sometimes fostered by the later medieval and Tudor authorities responsible for performances.

Chester is lucky in having lost only one of its recorded plays, and in possessing unusually full, if still hard to interpret, records of performances. These range from legal squabbles as to who was entitled to the best seats for the performances that took place in the Chester streets, to lists of expenses run up by the performers. (Beer figures largely on these, a fact which, like the authorities' continually worries about expense and possible bad behaviour, will strike a chord with amateur and professional theatre groups today.) The play that is lost was The Assumption of the Virgin, suppressed like other plays on Marian subjects, at the beginning of the Reformation. The whole cycle was eventually to fall victim to a changing religious climate. The loss of The Assumption (the York play on the same subject was given an exciting and moving production as part of the National Theatre's recent presentation of a composite cycle, The Mysteries) is doubly intriguing as it was presented by 'the Wives'; who these were, and whether they actually acted is not known. As it is the recorded performances point to all male casts.

A summary of the evidence for the history of the cycle, as collected by its most recent editors, Mills and Lumiansky, would suggest the following short history.

The first evidence for religious plays in Chester is of a performance on Corpus Christi day, a feast that normally falls in June, in 1422. Every year representatives of the guilds walked in procession behind the host (bread consecrated and so, according to Catholic doctrine, mysteriously 'become' the body of Christ, the Corpus Christi), holding torches, in the kind of ritual known as a 'light'. By the early years of the next century, theatrical performances to accompany this feast seem to have involved plays on all the subjects now covered, plus the Wives' play.

At around this time, the performances were shifted to Whitsuntide, the feast of the Holy Spirit that falls seven Sundays after Easter, eleven days before Corpus Christi, though the procession of lights seems to have continued. Although we don't know how and where earlier versions of the cycle were performed, we know that the Whitsun plays were performed on moveable stages, probably decorated wagons and carts, which stopped, in sequence, at different points in the city and repeated the play at each. First stop was the Abbey Gates, then the High Cross before St. Peter's church, then down into the city to Watergate Street and then Bridge Street. This performance was announced some time before by the reading of 'Banns' around the city, by a herald probably accompanied by some of the actors in costume. Each guild would spend lavishly on preparing its own particular 'carriage'.

The final performance was in 1575. We don't know how often or how regularly the plays were performed before then, though it does seem that the surviving texts derive from an attempt to overhaul the plays into a coherent and carefully argued whole. The necessity for this was religious and political, not simply aesthetic. The plays seem to have been given their most ambitious performances in the early days of Henry VIII's reformation, involving alterations in the text to emphasise biblical authority rather than sacramental mystery, and cutting down the amount of attention paid to Mary. Though what we have is not a specifically protestant cycle, it does take into account the pressures of religious change, and is to that extent a product of the Reformation. These pressures, coming both from Elizabeth's government, and from non co-operating protestant guilds, finally put an end to the cycle.

The cycle was far from being the only theatrical activity in medieval and Tudor Chester. There is evidence of many secular shows, interludes, plays and processions. Two of these in particular may have fed into the cycle. One recorded 'triumph' or ceremonial show, was a play of Aeneas, the founder of Rome, and his lover, Queen Dido of Carthage. It was written jointly by a local 'gentleman' and a 'master of Art', and was performed in the summer of 1563 with spectacular visual effects. This suggests an interest in Chester's Roman links, and a local interest in the theatrical presentation of history to parallel the inclusion of historical 'Roman' material in the cycle. But the major festival, of which this may have been a part, was a 'Midsummer Watch'. The games, plays and entertainments of which this consisted can only be surmised, but it is possible that some of the figures in the cycle - Gobbet, the Ale Wife, the Devils - bear some relation to these secular summer celebrations. Later traditions claim that the Midsummer Watch and the cycle alternated annually, but there is no real evidence for this. But when the cycle was suppressed it was replaced by an annual version of the Watch - a cleaned up version, under much stricter civic control.

Authors and Authority

Who wrote the Chester plays? Peter Happe, in the introduction to his Penguin volume of Mystery Plays, claims that 'the cycle is characterized by few hints of individual genius'. Whether or not this is true, it seems to be a red herring. Medieval plays were not written by individual geniuses, any more than medieval cathedrals were built by them. The Chester plays represent a corporate achievement. Their material was brought in from various sources, and at some point revised into a more unified and coherent whole. But this does not mean that it is in origin naive or improvised work. A historical summary of what we know of its origins and contexts suggest the kind of material that may have fed into it, but they also suggest a centralised control over its meaning and purpose.

Later traditions about the cycle do claim however that one Ranulf Higden was the author, a monk at the Abbey in the early fourteenth century, and author of a celebrated devotional work. Taken at face value, this would suggest an unusually early date for the cycle, but there is nothing to substantiate this. It seems that it is a later fiction, to make the cycle seem older than it is, and to give it a respectable religious provenance. The sixteenth and seventeenth century antiquaries who ascribed the cycle to Higden wanted an author for the same reasons as we often do when we talk about 'individual genius'; because they wanted an authority, an individual agency behind the text who guarantees its value. But for the early Tudor reviser of the plays, that authority was already in them - the authority of the Bible, and ultimately that of God. The plays continually explore this - characters refer back to prophecies they remember, or, like Herod's Doctor, to those in books, in order to interpret 'authoritatively' what they see. Christ's actions, as he himself explains, and God's interventions in the Old Testament, are all 'signs' that spell out the meaning of man's redemption. In watching the plays we are 'reading back' the phenomena of human history, in order to uncover the 'message' of the author of mankind. The confrontation between God's authority, as embodied in Christ, and human power, is the central conflict of the cycle.

The translation and the text

As a brief historical summary makes clear it is impossible to talk of an 'original' text of the cycle. When the guilds themselves do so, they mean the official copy, from which they wrote down the play assigned to them. The strict eye kept on this 'original' was not to make sure it always stayed the same, but rather the opposite - that it was always open to censorship and revision along current religious and political lines. By the time we have records of the plays, they exist under a centralised control of this sort, and the cycle had become an officially supervised civic event. The unity of style of the plays points not so much to an 'original' author, as to one man or a group, commissioned to overhaul a varied collection of plays, all dating from different periods, some indigenous, some based on plays from elsewhere. The result is a cycle with a unified verbal style, and a uniquely careful and complex historical and theological structure. A mass of heterogenous material has been formed at some point, probably in the 1530s, into a epic drama of the history of the world, from creation to doomsday. At this later stage of the cycle the texts of individual plays were controlled by their relation to this 'original'.

So no translator can speak of getting close of the 'original' cycle plays. I will use the term 'original' in its looser modern sense when talking about production style, but it should be clear by now that when I do so I refer to the pre-reformation history of the text generally. Even the 1530s 'original' disappeared, and we are reliant on texts copied for seventeenth century antiquaries, possibly, though not conclusively, from the official text. Any version of a line is chosen by comparing these existing texts against one another. In the end it may not even make much sense to talk of a 'translation'. In a way, I could think of myself as the latest of the Chester scribes, working with an idea of fidelity to a long standing tradition with the aim of preserving it (and with patrons who, like the Tudor council, have an eye on civic profit as much as on public instruction), but also fitting it to the requirements of my own audience. So the plays may be cut down and reshaped, but the overall proportions must be those of the texts I work from. The language must be updated, but only to make traditional ideas more comprehensible. This is like translation, but it is less like it than it is like the business of gradual reshaping and adaptation that was the life of the texts till they were frozen into a fixed form by Elizabethan suppression and seventeenth century antiquarianism. Whether translation or adaptation, I do, I hope, restore more of the existing material than other existing playing versions of this or other cycles. (The excellent Tony Harrison text, for the National Theatre Mysteries, is of course a personal composite of several cycles.) A misplaced sense of piety, whether to religious or to some imaginary idea of Merrie England and its charmingly naive artisan culture, has obscured and deformed too many versions. The only valid piety is a respect for the plays' theatrical life.

The language of my version should be comprehensible to a contemporary audience without being identifiably 'modern'. Many colloquial expressions remain the same, and the simpler archaisms are still familiar to us from hymns and carols. I have imitated the sixteenth century verse forms of the recorded text. The range of language may surprise those who expect modern (or victorian) piety, but it is true to the manuscript texts, and reflects the directness of players presenting not what they wished to appear holy, but what they believed to be true. I have clarified or occasionally simplified points of theological argument, but not suppressed them or tried to update them to currently held Christian beliefs. (Perhaps here I become unlike the Chester scribes of the past.) The whole structure and action of the plays is governed by ideas which, though foreign to most of us (even if we are Christians we are not sixteenth century Christians) are given a vivid theatrical life. We need no more assent to their stated beliefs to be excited by them than we need to be Marxists to enjoy a Brecht play - but like a Brecht play they should stimulate us to think what we do assent to, and why.

The structure of this version

To fit the plays into three parts of ordinary modern length necessarily involves cutting within particular plays, and cutting some plays out altogether. This reshaping also allows one to tailor the plays discreetly for the kinds of groups involved, and to avoid less obviously comprehensible material. It is in this last aim that most pitfalls lie. I have retained the often grotesque comedy of the plays, and as much as could be made clear of their theological argument. Modernized versions often prune away the most distinctive aspects of these plays in order to fit them to a modern expectation of religious drama, or to an equally modern 'workerist' piety as to the homespun sincerity (etc.) of the plays. So Maurice Hussey's version of the Nativity cuts out the Roman Emperor and his Sybil, as well as the comic midwives who submit Mary to an undignified virginity test. Tony Harrison's version also makes no use of such figures. But these characters on the fringes of events, their response to the unfolding of God's scheme and their discovery of its meaning, are precisely where the point of the Chester cycle, and much of its theatrical energy, can be seen to lie.

I have reshaped the material preserved in the early seventeenth century texts as follows. Play I of Lucifer, and the first half of play II, Adam and Eve, have been put together to make one play, Creation and Fall. (I have divided this in the current text into two episodes, one dealing with Lucifer, the other with Adam and Eve.) The second half of play II becomes Cain and Abel. Cuts in these plays are local, mainly within speeches. The same is true of III and IV, Noah's Flood and Abraham and Isaac, whose structure remains very much the same. I have omitted play V, Balaam and Balaak. The second half of the first evening begins with The Nativity (play VI in the original), from which I have cut the episode with Elizabeth, and the Doctor's long interpretation of the Roman scenes. The Shepherds play, (VII) is cut within speeches only. The last play of the first evening, Magi and Innocents is a compressed version of plays VIII, IX and X, heavily cut, but losing no episode completely.

The Purification, play XI, is cut completely, the second evening beginning with The Temptation (XII), Lazarus (XIII), and Judas (XIV). All these are cut but not restructured, as is the Last Supper (XV), played after the interval. To end the evening Jesus's journey to Calvary, from the Passion (play XVII), is grafted on to The Trial (XVI) to be played on the streets outside the Abbey. Some, but not all, of this material is recapped at the beginning of the third evening. In this final part, The Passion is followed by the Harrowing of Hell (XVII) and The Resurrection (XVIII), all quite lightly cut. The first play after the interval compresses the Journey to Emmaus and Doubting Thomas and the Ascension (XVIII and XIX) into one account of the appearance of the risen Jesus to his apostles, and after a short interlude based on Pentecost (XXI), The Judgement (XXIV) follows, in a cut version that differs mainly in making the damned and saved souls less specific. The opening speech of Lazarus is then recapped as an epilogue. Antichrist (XXIII) and his prophets (XXII) have been cut completely.

The handful of plays omitted are among the most complex and intriguing of the cycle, but not perhaps the most immediate to a modern audience. Our version pays less attention than does the recorded sixteenth century text to the prophecies promising Christ, and to the aftermath of his resurrection and ascension. This material seemed comparatively expendable in an attempt to combine a practicable playing time with as much of the character of the plays as recorded as was possible. Anyone wishing to use part of this text for their own production, could, of course, make their own selection of the eighteen episodes for an evening length, or shorter, presentation. The shortest of the plays (discounting the penultimate 'interlude') should last ten minutes, the longest, thirty.

Characters and Casting

Every guild would provide its own actors for its own individual play. Some of these would be amateur, some professional, in so far as we can tell from lists of the expenses that the guilds incurred. This might be reflected in the demands that different roles make. Some seem to suggest professional entertainers, others well-known local 'stars' like Absalon in Chaucer's Miller's Tale (an enthusiastic Herod). Others again call for less 'technical' but more intellectual qualities in the actor. But there would not be 'star' roles linking across the plays. Each guild would have its own God, its own Jesus, and so on.

Our approach reproduces many of the conventions, and we hope the effects, of this kind of presentation. Amateurs and professionals work together, even within particular groups, and the cast includes a whole range of ages, backgrounds and kinds of involvement in drama necesary to present so wide ranging and inclusive a theatrical spectacle. God and our link figure, 'Gobbet' are played by the same actors throughout, but other figures are played by different actors each time they appear. This has the effect of suggesting that no particular actor has to 'be' Christ - 'impersonations' of Jesus are always disappointing - but that our cast as a group is telling his story, representing him and the other figures when called upon to do so, representing them as a guild player might, not trying to 'be' them, as would a modern naturalistic actor.

The question of acting convention is too large to go into here, and perhaps not really relevant - the style we arrive at will necessarily be a mixture, as the plays themselves span so many kinds of characters and such different situations. But the question of convention does have some relevance in explaining this text to anyone who might consider using it, or any other version of a medieval play, for their own productions. No one can reproduce the style(s) the plays were originally acted in. Even if we could we probably couldn't follow or enjoy the result. But some experimentation with conventional and formalized styles of presentation distant from our normal diet of T.V. naturalism is necessary simply to make theatrical sense of the plays as written. I have not tried to translate these plays into a modern staging convention, and so to that extent present them as problems for groups and their directors to solve. No solution will be 'right' if historical accuracy is our criterion, but any could be, if it made the plays work.

Some notes on individual characters

There are nine 'orders' of Angels. They are named in the cast list of the Creation and Fall play, in which a representative of each order speaks. Angels exist in multiples of nine, three times three, the number of the Trinity. Though the Chester plays show an interest in number and pattern, they are not so clear on the hierarchical structure of the orders. Lucifer is head of his order, of which Lightborn is a lowlier member. Those who fall with them to Hell all belong to Lucifer's order, and have acted with, or almost as a part of him. All the devils are thus in a sense aspects of Lucifer/Satan, just as all the angels within one order exist as one; they can become many to fulfill God's commands - like the four Cherubim who guard Eden at the end of that play.

In relation to human figures, or in particular stories, the angels acquire names and individual identities - Gabriel, for example, in the Nativity, or Michael in the Harrowing of Hell. If all the angels in Nativity are played by one actor, 'Gabriel', then he/she/it becomes almost the most important figure in the play. This is one way of doing it, but they it is equally possible to have a different actor present 'the angel' on each appearance. This has the practical advantage of allowing more people to be involved, and it also puts across the essentially indivisible nature of the angels, as members of a perfect pattern of orders, and their asexuality, as neither male nor female, and so actable as both. Our practise tends more to the options offered by the second alternative, with the addition of using our narrator/compere figure, Gobbet on the Green to take over some angelic interventions. Angels have a number of functions, of which the most neutral, that of simply getting people from place to place, seemed to suit our master of ceremonies.

Gobbet on the Green is the name of the messenger who introduces the original Abraham and Isaac play (play IV). The relevant verse is transferred in this version to the beginning of the cycle. Gobbet retains the meaning today of piece, or fragment, but it can also mean, as Mills and Lumiansky point out in their commentary on the cycle 'Go fast' ('bet' meaning 'fast'). The name seems to suggest a folk figure, perhaps of the kind that might turn up in the Midsummer Watch, but there is no real evidence for this. All the 'messenger' figures in the cycle make comic claims for their speed, and have an obviously more clown-like and crowd-pleasing approach to the audience than the 'Doctors' and 'Expositors' who turn up to point to the significance of what we have seen. There is no reason why both explanations of the name may not be to some extent true. Whoever he is, Gobbet belongs to that class of clown-like functionaries who recur in the plays - Octavian's messenger, Herod's 'pretty Pratt', even Lucifer's deputy, Lightborn.

We have expanded the role to meet a practical demand - that of co-ordinating a large number of plays with separate casts, and of (brief pause in the writing to touch wood!) coping with the unexpected during the performance. Clearing crowds, announcing players, maybe even keeping the peace would all be part of the function of these figures in the busy street-theatre context of the original productions. New Gobbet material comes from the 'Banns', or by incorporating other roles - the Doctors and Expositors, where we have kept them, the more neutral 'traffic control' angels, or the occasional human figure who fulfills the same function. All these changes are marked against the name of the original character in the text of the relevant play. Finally in our short penultimate play, we have broadened the role by using some of the material of the original Pentecost (play XXI). Here, Gobbet acts as a representative of the audience, asking for guidance, to interpret and believe in what we have seen. So despite his functions on stage, his occasional helpful interventions in the action, our Gobbet is essentially a bridge to the audience, an entertainer, an explainer, and finally a kind of everyman.

A different kind of textual problem is set by the figure of Mary Magdalen. In the Lazarus play (our play 9, XIII in the original cycle) Mary, the sister of Martha appears. In some medieval traditions she is identified with the woman who turns up at the banquet at the house of Simon the Leper, to repent her life as a prostitute and wash Jesus's feet (our play 10, original XIV). So which Mary is the Mary Magdalen who attends at the Crucifixion and Resurrection?

Unlike other medieval dramatic traditions, the Chester cycle does not clearly identify the two women, any more than the gospel accounts do. In no other play of the cycle is there any sense that Mary the sister of Martha is a repentant prostitute, and the woman at Simon's house is not named by anyone in the play, and seems a stranger to them, in all but reputation. So it seems better to see that woman as a separate role, and take Mary the sister of Martha to be the Mary who mourns at the Crucifixion, and who is the first to meet the risen Jesus. Perhaps the uncertainty in the surviving Chester text marks an attempt to de-emphasize the role of a popular Catholic saint, parallel to its suppression of the 'Wives" play of the Assumption of the Virgin. In any case, another production might well want to combine the two figures in order to produce a strong female role. This would not contradict medieval tradition - as the National Theatre production's re-assignment of the scene after the Resurrection to Mary the Mother of God most certainly did.

Unnamed characters (first and second citizen, and so on) tend to come in fours, and always speak in order - first, then second and so on. How far this represents a formalized stage convention (are they meant to be as disciplined and unrealistic in their presentation as a Greek chorus, or as we may assume the angels to be?) or whether it is a convention in which the texts were written down, the actors splitting up the speeches in rehearsal as they wished, is impossible to ascertain. Like many other things in the text, this is best resolved by the performing group. The same applies to an always vexed question in amateur drama - the disproportion of male roles to female. Even assuming we don't present a full complement of apostles in each separate cast there are still vastly more speaking roles for men than for women - 95 to 32 in our version. A further 77 roles are ambiguous, whether as asexual beings - angels, devils - or simply unspecified - the damned, the saved, the torturers, and so on. God I have counted as male -still a debatable point theologically, but so specified in the cycle. Angels and devils we have cast as either sex, and used some of the leeway given in unnamed roles to introduce roles for women.   But it is worth returning here to the question of acting styles. With a stylized mode of production there seems no reason why all roles should not be interchangeably male or female. Our own practise adopts this kind of convention in some instances, and other productions might well develop this further.

Places and stage directions

The dialogue of the plays is usually careful and explicit in indicating the action it requires. Every action has precise meaning and clear consequences. This points to a visually striking but unfussy mode of presentation, in which action and word are equally significant, and one accompanies the other without rendering it redundant.   In consequence the plays present complex events, and invite us to interpret and respond to them, by means of a notably concise and clear cut style of theatrical story-telling. There seems little need for extensive stage directions as such.   Those that exist in the manuscripts often seem more like narrative captions - such as might be projected during a Brecht play - than instructions to the actors or notes on the staging. I have added a few extra directions (marked in square brackets) with the same aim of clarifying a section of narrative. Like the original directions, these indicate the action a particular set of lines refer to, without pushing the actors towards any particular way of staging it, or any particular interpretation.

Some of my stage directions expand a little on the original in one particular - the identification of place. However the plays were originally staged - and this would not in any case remain stable over the plays pre-reformation history - many of them present action in one, two or even three discrete locations.   The characters move from one of these places to another with unrealistic speed. Mary goes from Bethany to Galilee to fetch Jesus by going across the stage. The action itself is seamless - a convention is adopted by which time and space are compressed. This may seem simple, even childlike, but the cycle plays develop it as a flexible way in which to present an action that is both in human time and timeless - whose central importance is the impingment of God's scheme of things on human time and place. God, the risen Jesus, the angels and devils can be anywhere - they come and go in contradiction to the human sense of space and time, itself continually reiterated in the plays' map-like precision about who is where when. Perhaps it makes more sense of the staging conventions of the plays to think of them as a kind of map of cosmic events.   They necessarily compress events of an infinite vastness into representations limited by time and space, but they aim to do so accurately and in proportion, as a kind of diagram, or model. When, in the <u>Nativity,</u> the emperor Octavian, far away in Rome, can <u>see</u> the Christ child, by virtue of the grace God grants a pagan prophetess, the two contrasted worlds, of pagan splendour and Christian humility, come together in the same limited playing space. Rule over the laws of space is ultimately in God's hands, as are the rules of time, and at the incarnation, when God, as Jesus becomes man, human reality and God's reality intersect. This is the kind of effect, the magic if you like, that a 'simple' playing style makes possible.

The latest scholarly edition of the complete cycle is that of R. M. Lumiansky and David Mills, published by the Early English Text Society in 1974. Their commentary followed in 1986 and they have also edited a volume of documentary evidence for the cycle, <u>The Chester Mystery Cycle; Essays and Documents</u> (University of North Carolina Press, 1983). All the available documentary records of theatrical performances in Chester (to 1640) are collected in <u>Records of Early English Drama: Chester</u> ed. Lawrence M. Clopper, (Manchester University Press, 1979).

I am indebted to all these volumes for the factual material contained in the introduction; any errors are mine, I'm sure, not theirs.

Thanks to David Mills and Nick Davis of Liverpool University for their encouragements and advice; to Pat Brooksbank and Cathy Rees for typing the first version of the performance text and revising it for publication, respectively; and to Robin Bloxsidge for giving it a smooth run through the press.

Thanks finally to Carolyn Fleming, for putting up with endless requests for rhyme words (among other strange noises), and of course for much else.

Edward Burns

ACKNOWLEDGEMENT

This acting text has drawn on a number of published editions of The Chester Mystery Cycle and, in particular, its preparation has involved the use of the following in which copyright is held by the Early English Text Society:

> The Chester Plays, Vol. I, re-edited from the MSS by Hermann Deimling, London, Kegan Paul, Trench, Trübner and Co. for the Early English Text Society, 1892.

> The Chester Plays, Vol. II, re-edited from the MSS by Dr. Matthews, London, Kegan Paul, Trench, Trübner and Co. and Oxford University Press for the Early English Text Society, 1916.

> The Chester Mystery Cycle, Vol. I: Text, edited by R. M. Lumiansky and David Mills, London, Oxford University Press for the Early English Text Society, 1974.

Liverpool University Press is grateful to the Early English Text Society for permission to publish work based on the Society's editions.

PART ONE
The Coming of Christ

GOBBET:

All peace, and hearken to our play.
Gobbet on the Green must have his say -
If you will give us time and space
To tell you our story.
For we will show you here today
God's will to man, now and always,
As has been acted on many a day
Here in this city.
Dancers and musicians of this town
Shall show you the heavenly mansion -
All the orders of angels, and their creation,
Done to their very best.
And when the angels are made,
All bright and clear,
Then follows the fall of Lucifer.
To bring that off and win a cheer,
Our actors will be hard pressed.

Then the set builders, the makers of properties,
Will see that Paradise is ready.
Bring out the snake and the apple tree,
For Adam, and lady Eve.
The tale they tell is the tale of our woe,
For if Adam had not sinned so,
We had been happy, long ago.
Watch this, and believe.

PLAY 1
Creation and Fall

CAST:

God
Lucifer
Angel
Archangel
Lightborn [an angel of Lucifer's order]
Virtues
Cherubim
Dominations
Principalities
Thrones
2 Devils (Lucifer and Lightborn)
Adam
Eve
Adder
Four Cherubim

I

THE CREATION OF THE ANGELS AND THE FALL OF LUCIFER

GOD:

Ego sum alpha et omega,
Primus et novissimus.
It is my will it should be so;
It is, it was, it shall be thus.

I am great God gracious,
Which never had beginning.
All the mirth of the majesty
Is magnified in me.
I am the truth of the Trinity,
Which never shall be twinning.
I was never but one
And ever one in Three.
Prince principal, proved
In my perpetual providence.
All bliss is in my building
Exalted by my excellence.
As God gracious and glorious
All power lies in me.

Now since I sit here so solemn,
So set in my habitation,
A blissful light here will I build
A heaven without ending.
I cast round a comely compass

In comely creation
Nine orders of angels
Be ever at once defending.
Do your best endeavour, and doubt you not
That under my domination
You sit in celestial safety.
All joy to you here attending.
Love is my lordship
Light my law's foundation.
Through the might of my majesty
Your mirth shall be ever amending.

LUCIFER:

Lord, in grace and might thou hast us wrought.
Nine orders of angels, as each may see.
Cherubin and Seraphim made in a thought,
Thrones and Dominations in bliss to be.

Principalities, that order bright,
Powers, to live in blissful light,
Virtues great, in thy great might,
Angels and archangels.

Nine orders are present here to thee,
That thou hast made full right.
In thy bliss all bright we be,
And I am their leader lord, here in thy sight.

GOD:

I made you all in heavenly might.
Nine orders of angels, great in their beauty,
Each one with the others, as it is right,
To walk about the Trinity.

Now Lucifer and Lightborn, look that you lowly be.
See the blessing of beginning on my first operation.
In craft and cunning, cast not past comprehension,
Exalt you not your excellence in excess of exaltation.
See you act wisely. I must go from your sight.
The world is void and vacant.   From light let it take
      formation,
With a dungeon deep under that never knows light.
This work is well wrought. My light is its formation.
This work is made mighty. It shines out clean and clear.
As I made you from nothing, my blessing I give you here.

ANGELS:

We thank you, Lord of sovereignty
That made us all so clean and clear.
Always in bliss to abide with thee.
Grant us the grace to live well here.

ARCHANGELS:

May that peerless prince to us all grant grace
To please him always and give good cheer.
Let us give him thanks for making this place.
Let us sing him a song here.

[The angels sing. God speaks to Lucifer and Lightborn]

GOD:

Now that I see I have formed you so fair,
Exalted you to such excellence.
I sit you here right next to my chair,
My love to you is so fervent.
Look out - see you fall not into despair,
Or all your beauty will disappear.
Your pride shall have its fall, by your own intent.

LUCIFER:

Nay Lord, never will we do that deed.
Nothing could make us do wrong to thee.
Thy godhead great fills us all with dread.
We could never exalt ourselves so high.
Thou hast put thy mark on us, by might and by main,
In thy bliss forever to abide and to be,
In lasting life our life to lead.
As the bearer of light, lord, thou made me.

LIGHTBORN:

And I am made of the self-same mould,
Living in love of our creator,
The great God that made us gayer than gold.
In the light of his diadem we ever endure.

GOD:

I forbid you both to come more near.
You know your station - see you keep it.
The covenant I charge you with, see that you hold,
Or heaven you forfeit.

For I must go, my track retrace,
Take stock of my bliss from tower to tower.
Each one of you stay here, stand still in your place.
Lucifer, I make you governor.
I charge you all, by the grounds of my grace,
That all stay put, in pattern of order.
Behold the beams of my bright face,
Which ever was and is and will endure.
Your health and your holiness, in every case,
Is this - to behold your creator.
There was never one like me, none so full of grace,
Nor ever shall be one, to shine so in light.
I will be with you for ever, here in this place,
The comfort of angels, their bliss full bright.
You will see me again in the shortest space.
It is my will to return within this hour.

The angels sing. God withdraws.

LUCIFER:

Aha, I am wondrous bright,
I shine among you all full clear.
Alone in heaven I bear the light,
And so I would if God were here.
All I need is to sit right there.
Were I on his throne I were wise as he.
What do you say, all you angels here.
Some support now let me see.

VIRTUES:

We have no part of your great pride.
Our hearts cannot harbour such a thought.
Our lord shall always be our guide,
And keep us safe whom he hath wrought.

CHERUBIM:

Our lord commanded all that are here
To keep to their seats, both greater and less.
And so I warn you, Lucifer,
Your pride will turn to great distress.

LUCIFER:

Distress - I command you all to cease
And see the beauty that I bear.
All heaven shines in my brightness.
For God himself shines not so clear.

DOMINATIONS:

Of all the angels you bear the prize.
All of us in beauty you surpassed.
I advise you now, you must be wise,
Or you will find yourself bound fast.

PRINCIPALITIES:

Be wise, be careful what you do.
You will be thrown from heaven, far out cast,
And any one who follows you
Your pride will ever blast.

CHERUBIM:

Our brothers counsel is good to hear.
So I say to you Lucifer and Lightborn,
Avoid the throne, go not so near
We meet your pride with scorn.

LIGHTBORN:

In faith brother, you shall
Sit in this throne - you are clean and clear,
You are as wise after all
As God himself if he were here.
So I say you should be sat here
For all heaven to behold.
The bright light of thy body clear
Shines brighter than God's, a thousandfold.

THRONES:

Let that wish pass clean out of thy thought.
Cast away all wicked pride.
Keep the brightness where you were wrought
Let the lord be your only guide.

POWERS:

Pride alas is the curse of beauty.
It turns your thought to great offence.
The brightness of your fair body
Will take you from hence.

LUCIFER:

Will take me hence? Look lords, look, on every side,
All on me, all turn your eyes.
I order all angels, far and wide,
To look on what I do here.

Greater than God am I glorified.
I stand right here. I know no fear.
I am the peerless prince of pride.
God's light shines not so bright and clear.

Here will I sit now, here in his stead.
To exalt myself for all to see.
Behold my body, my hands, my head.
The might of God is marked on me.
All angels, turn, do as I've said,
Kneel to your sovereign, bow down your knee.
I am your comfort, your lord and your head,
The mirth and might of majesty.

LIGHTBORN: And I am next, in the same degree,
                        Full of the same bright excellence.
                        I think if I might sit him by,
                        All heaven would do us reverence.
                        All the orders of angels must obey thee and me.
                        You have turned them with your eloquence.
                        If we stood next to the Trinity
                        We'd outshine him with our brilliance.

DOMINATIONS: Why do you do this great offence?
                        Lucifer and Lightborn, hear what I say -
                        Our sovereign Lord will send you hence
                        If he finds you making this affray.

                        Go to your seats. Get you hence.
                        Right dangerous is the game you play.
                        You'll soon find out the consequence.
                        Your dance leads on a wicked way.

LUCIFER: I say to you all - do me reverence.
                        I am full of heavenly grace.
                        God might come, but I won't go hence.
                        I'll sit right here before his face.

[Lucifer sits in God's throne. God returns]

GOD: Lucifer, who put you here when I was gone?
                        What offence have I done to thee?
                        I made you my friend, and you are my foe.
                        Why have you trespassed this way against me?
                        Above all the angels none other sat, none other so,
                        Right near to my great majesty.

                        Tell me, what are you doing here?
                        Who is your prince and principal?
                        I made thee an angel, Lucifer,
                        And thou would be lord of all.
                        Therefore I charge thee and thy fellows here -
                        Fast from this place fall.
                        Soon enough I'll change your cheer.
                        Your foul pride sends you to Hell

Lucifer and Lightborn fall [and re-appear as first and second devil.]

FIRST DEVIL: Alas that ever we were wrought,
                      To come at last to this dark place.
                      We were in joy, now all becomes naught.
                      Alas, we forfeit all our grace.

SECOND DEVIL: By you to the pit we both were brought.
                      You dashed us down to a dungeon base.
                      You found us sorrow when joy we sought.
                      The devil's speed to your stinking face.

FIRST DEVIL: My face, false traitor - treat me fair.
                      It was you who lead us both astray.
                      I'm encumbered in cankers, I'm kindled in care,
                      I sink in sorrow - what can I say?

SECOND DEVIL: You brought us along this wicked way,
                      Through thy might and through thy pride,
                      Out of the bliss that lasts always,
                      In sorrow for ever now to abide.

FIRST DEVIL: Your wit lead us on as well as mine.
                      Your pride provoked you, you showed your scorn.
                      Now here we are in the fire of hell pain.
                      Down until doomsday these blasts can burn.

SECOND DEVIL: Then can we never fly our woe.
                      We lie down here, two fiends devil-black.
                      Alas that we forgot him so,
                      The lord of love that did us make.

FIRST DEVIL: And therefore shall I, for his sake,
                      Show mankind my great envy.
                      As soon as ever he can him make,
                      I shall be out, man to destroy.

SECOND DEVIL: Out alas, where is the might
                      That we so strong did show?
                      In heaven we bore so great a light,
                      Who now in Hell lie low.

FIRST DEVIL: Out alas, for wickedness
                      I fast am bound in woeful cheer.
                      Never away can any pass
                      From Hell, they lie forever here.

GOD: Ah wicked pride, deserving woe.
                      My mirth thou hast made amiss.
                      I suffer much. I did not will it so.
                      I wanted them still in bliss.
                      Ah, pride, why might thou not burst in two?
                      Why did they that? Why do they thus?
                      See all you angels, see, pride is your foe,

All sorrow shall follow wherever it is.

Though they have broken my commandment,
I suffer for them, full sorrowfully.
But yet fulfill I my intent.
That which I thought, so do I.
All my three persons are at one assent
A solemn matter now to try.
To make man in our image have I always meant.
Through his own seed will he multiply.

As I have made you all from nought,
At my own wishing,
My first day here have I wrought,
I give it my blessing.

II

THE CREATION AND THE FALL OF ADAM AND EVE

GOD:

I God, most in majesty,
I in whom no beginning nor end may be,
Now Heaven and earth is made by me.
But earth lie all in darkness.
At my bidding, let there be light.

Light is good, I see in sight.
The light is day, the darkness night.
This, the first day, do I bless.

Now will I make a firmament,
Over the water to be bent,
To make division permanent,
And stand above always.
With waters above and waters below,
Forever it will my power show.
Heaven I call it, for all to know,
On this, the second day.

Now will I gather the waters all.
By the name of 'seas' men shall them call.
The dryness 'earth'. And so they shall
Be known by everyone.
On earth all herbs and grass will spring,
Each the seed of its own kind bearing
Each tree a different fruit will bring.
The third day now is come and gone.

Now will I make through my might
Two lights in the heaven bright.
The sun for day, the moon for night
For light that men might see.
Stars I make, by my intent,
And fix them in the firmament.

I see my work is excellent,
The fourth day pleases me.

Now from the waters fish will I bring,
Fowls in the firmament flying
Great whales in the sea swimming.
I make them all in a thought.
Beasts and fowls, fruit stone and tree.
These works are good, as I can see.
All beasts, go forth and multiply.
Complete what I have wrought.

Five days now are past and gone.
All beasts will I bring forth on the earth anon,
Creeping or flying, every one
According to its kind.
Now it is done at my bidding.
Beasts running flying and creeping.
All my work is to my liking,
That is what I find.

He goes to the place where he creates Adam

Now heaven and earth is made express,
Make we man in our likeness.
Fish fowl and beast, the greater and the less,
To master them he has the might.
In our shape I make thee.

Man and woman will thou be.
Grow and multiply shall ye,
All earth is thine by right.
To help thee thou shall have here
The herbs and trees in seed and fruit together.
All shall be in thy power,
All the beasts also.
All on earth living
All in sea swimming
All in air flying
All keep you safe from woe.

Now this is done - I see that right.
All things are made, all through my might.
The sixth day here in my sight
Is much the best.
Heaven and earth is made complete
With all that needs to be on it.
Tomorrow on the seventh day, as is fit,
From work I take my rest.

Man now have I made.
The spirit of life must enter his clay.

Adam rises

Rise up Adam, rise up, rise.

A man full of soul and life,
And come with me to paradise.
Remember this. Be wise.

God takes Adam to Paradise. They stand in front of the tree of knowledge.

GOD: Here, Adam. I give thee this place,
                To be thy comfort and thy peace.
                Keep it well, for yours it is.
                Do as I say.
                Of all the trees that be herein
                You may eat the fruit and do no sin,
                But woe from this tree will you win.
                Eat of it not, in no way.

                The time you eat the fruit of this tree
                You earn your death, believe you me.
                Fearful, I tell you, must you be.

God takes Adam by the hand and makes him lie down. He takes a rib out of his side.

GOD: It is not good for man to be alone.
                Asleep thou art, well I see,
                I take from thee a bone.
                I make of it a help for thee.
                Flesh of thy flesh with a heart that's free.

God makes the woman from Adam's rib. Adam wakes.

ADAM: Ah, Lord, where have I been?
                Since I slept much have I seen.
                Wonders saw I in my dream.
                Things I cannot tell.

GOD: Rise up Adam and awake.
                Here have I made for thee a mate.
                Thou her and she to thee must take.
                Call her what you will.

Adam rises.

ADAM: Well I see Lord, through thy grace
                From bone of my bone created she was,
                Flesh of my flesh - my shape she has.
                'Virago' I call her, 'taken-from-man'.
                For her kind all men will forsake
                Father and mother, and wives to them take.
                So two become one, as you did make
                Two, we two, woman and man.

Adam and Eve stand naked, without shame. The serpent comes out of a hole. The devil enters, walking.

DEVIL:

> Out, out, what sorrow is this,
> That I have lost so great a bliss?
> As soon as I thought to do amiss,
> Out of heaven I fell.
> The brightest angel was I before this,
> The brightest that was, that will be, that is.
> Pride cast me down - I tell you this -
> From heaven right down into Hell.
>
> Of earthly paradise now I see
> A man is master, made of clay.
> Should he have such bliss? I tell thee - nay.
> Watch me here awhile.
> I can teach his wife to play.
> I can lead them both astray.
> She will do anything I say.
> Their hopes will I beguile.
>
> From the tree of paradise,
> She will take fruit for her delight
> Women are greedy for anything nice.
> She won't resist.
> They will eat it, certainly,
> And then they will suffer, just like me,
> Banished from this valley,
> Banned from all their bliss.
>
> A manner of adder lives in this place.
> Wings like a bird it has,
>
> An adders feet, a maiden's face,
> Her shape will I take.
> So, by Beelzebub, I must be gone.
> The adders coat will I put on
> There's work today that must be done,
> As fast as ever I may.

[The Devil takes on the form of the serpent. The serpent speaks to Eve]

SERPENT:

> Woman, why was God so strict,
> To say that no fruit could be picked,
> When paradise by his own edict
> Is yours, to choose your meat?

EVE:

> No, the fruit of every tree
> His leave to pick and eat have we.
> But the fruit of this one we must flee.
> Of that we must not eat.
>
> This tree, that in the middle is,
> If we eat of that, we do amiss
> God said we should die for this
> For eating of that tree.

SERPENT:

> Woman, I tell you, believe not this.
> If you eat you lose no bliss,

Nor the joy that is his.
You will gain much more and be as wise as he.

God is subtle, wise in his wits
He knows well, when you eat it,
Your eyes will be unknit.
Like gods you both shall be.
You will know good and evil also.
Thats why he warned you, lest you should know.
You should have seen that he is your foe.
So, do after me.

Take the fruit and try.
It is good meat, I testify.
If you find I lie
Then say I am false.
You will know both wealth and woe.
You will be as gods, you two,
You and your husband also.
Take one apple, take no more.

EVE: Ah Lord, this tree is fair and bright
                Green and lovely in my sight.
                The fruit is sweet, great is its might,
                If gods of us it makes.
                One apple from it I will eat
                Just to try the meat.
                One small morsel must I keep
                For my husbands sake.

Eve takes the fruit from the serpent and eats some of it.

EVE: Adam, husband, my life, my dear,
                Eat some of this apple here.
                It tastes full fair, my darling dear,
                Eat it for my sake.

ADAM: That is true, Eve. I see it clear.
                The fruit is sweet and fine and fair.
                So in answer to your prayer –
                One morsel will I take.

Adam takes the fruit and eats some of it. He weeps.

ADAM: Out, alas, what ails me?
                I am naked. Cursed may thou be.
                I have broken, because of thee
                My Lord's commandment.

EVE: Alas, the adder has been right sly,
                Why did I do it, why did I?
                Naked we both are,
                Of our shape ashamed.

ADAM: I knew the truth. I prophesied,
                When you were taken from my side,

That woe to man would then betide -
So 'woman' were thou called.

EVE: Adam, husband, I say we take
Some fig leaves, for shames sake -
For our bodies some covering make
To hide us, thee and me.

ADAM: So, our bodies let us hide.
Under the tree will I abide.
God will come soon.
Then out of this place go we.

Adam and Eve cover their genitals with leaves. They hide under the trees. Music plays.

GOD: Adam, Adam, where art thou?

ADAM: Ah Lord, thy voice I hear,
I am naked, so I swear,
And so I hid.

GOD: Who told thee Adam Thou naked was?
Only thy trespass.
Of that tree thou eaten has,
As I forbid.

ADAM: Lord, the woman that is here,
The woman you gave me for help-mate dear,
She gave me part, it was at her prayer
That I did eat.

GOD: Woman, why did you do so?

EVE: The adder, Lord, she was my foe
She deceived me too.
She made me eat that meat.

GOD: On thy belly adder must thou go
And eat the earth. I curse thee so.
The woman always will be your foe,
For thy misdeed today.

And woman, I warn thee, the mastery,
Shall pass to men.
In his power you will be.
Your children will be born in misery,
Your lot is sorrow and pain.
And man - I say to thee -
Because thou hast not heeded me
Great trouble to thee will it be
On earth to get thy living.
Roots and herbs now must you eat

> Sorely must you strain and sweat
> With might and main to win your meat.
> It won't be to your liking.

ADAM:

> Alas, I was disobedient -
> I fell by woman's enticement.
> Who trusts to them, whatever his intent,
> Is bound to be deceived.

GOD:

> Dead beasts' skins must clothe thee.
> For death now is part of ye.
> Death may you never flee,
> Go where you will.

God puts garments made of animal skin on Adam and Eve.

GOD:

> Adam, you have your desire now.
> Of good and evil you would know.
> So it has fallen. Now must you go.
> Your desire is fulfilled.
>
> Out on the earth thou must begone.
> To work thy way to live thereon.
> There is nothing else now to be done.
> Go forth. And take Eve with thee.

God drives Adam and Eve out of paradise. Music plays.

GOD:

> My angels, I order you here to abide.
> With sharp swords on every side,
> To keep out man, who our will defied.
> My cherubim, guard this place.

FIRST ANGEL:

> We are here already Lord in thy sight,
> With flame of fire ready to fight
> Till Right and Wisdom, Mercy and Might,
> Take mankind back to grace.

SECOND ANGEL:

> No man by craft or greediness
> Can come back into paradise.
> After man was so unwise
> No more can he come there.

THIRD ANGEL:

> No man comes to this city.
> Swords of fire have all we
> To make man from this place to flee,
> That God build wondrous fair.

FOURTH ANGEL:

> Through his guilt mankind found woe
> And left this ground of grace.
> We fight against man, now God's foe,
> With fire we guard this place.

GOBBET: So now, good people, you have heard tell
               How Adam and Eve, our parents, fell.
               To live they must toil on the earth full well,
               As they from earth were made.
               Our actors, players from Davenham,
               Will tell of the children of Adam -
               How Cain was the first to kill a man,
               And Abel the first to know death.

PLAY 2

Cain and Abel

CAST: **Adam**
Eve
Cain
Abel
God

ADAM:

Lord God, highest King,
Who out of nothing made all things,
Birds beasts and the grass growing,
Who me from earth has made -
Give me grace to do thy bidding.
For after sorrow and suffering
Thou granted me a blessing -
Two sons to make me glad.

Cain and Abel, my children dear
Listen to me and you shall learn,
You who both begotten were
After your parents fall.
I slept while your mother created was.
The dream God sent to me in grace
I tell you sons face to face.
But I will not tell you all.

I know by things that I did see
That God will come from heaven on high
To overcome the devil sly
And come into mankind.
My blood for me his death will win,
The blood I forfeited in doing sin.
A new law shall he then begin.
So men shall rescue find.

Also I see, as I shall say,
That God will come on the last day
To judge all men as living clay
In flame of fire burning.
The good to heaven, the evil to hell -
To your children see this tale you tell.
I saw this in paradise before I fell,
As I lay sleeping.

Now will I say what you must do
To draw down Gods love unto you.
Cain - a husbandman's craft for you,
And Abel, a shepherd be.
The corn that grows all fair and clean

Stretching in rows as far as can be seen,
Cain, you shall offer, so I mean,
To God in majesty.

And Abel, while your life shall last,
See you offer - now do what I ask -
To God, the first born beast.
To do that are you bound.
That way you please the God of might
If you do it well and right,
With a heart that holy in his sight
And full devotion.
Now, how you get your sustenance
You can understand at once.
Since I knew that foul mischance
When I took the fruit to eat
My dearest children fair and free
With this spade that you can see
I have dug. Learn this from me -
Just so must you win your meat.

EVE:

My sweet children, my darlings dear,
Now you see how we live here,
All because we disobedient were,
And did what God forbade we should.
Of my monthly pain there had been no need.
That comes to remind me of my misdeed.
Nor did I need spin woollen thread
To keep us from the cold.

Another sorrow I suffer also.
My children must I bear in woe,
As I have done both you two.
And so shall women all.
It was the devil, our bitter foe
That made us all our joy forgo.
Please God, my sons, and sin not so,
That you may not so fall.

CAIN:

Now then Mother, I say to ye
A ploughman I am and so will I be.
My daddy has taught it all to me
I learnt all his lore.

He brings in his plough

Corn have I in plenty.
Great Sacrifice to God you'll see.
Soon I'll make sure he
Sends me plenty more.

ABEL:

And I will make, with devotion,
The sacrifice to which I'm bound.
The best of the beasts, by my crown,
For the lord will I choose.

I offer it before thee here,
Meekly in good manner.
No beast for thee can be too dear.
The best I'll gladly lose.

Adam and Eve go out

CAIN:
I am the eldest of us two,
So I must have the first go.
Some of the grain that's trampled low
Is good enough for him.
The standing corn, I say to thee
Was eaten by beasts as anyone can see.
God, you get no more from me,
Be you ever so grim.
By my prick, it's a waste of corn,
All the better ears to burn.
The stubbly corn will serve your turn,
Or the devil can string me up.

Lord, lord here may you see
Such corn as grew to me.
Part of it, all honestly,
Hereby for thee I fetch.
I hope you will honour me in this
And send me more of worldly bliss.
Else, forsooth, you do amiss,
And you'll be in my debt.

ABEL:
Now my brother as I see
Has done his sacrifice to thee.
I will offer, as befits me,
What thou to me hath sent.
The best beast, I say to thee,
In all my flock with heart free
Offered to thee now shall it be.
Receive, Lord, my present.

A flame descends on Abel's sacrifice

ABEL:
Ah high God and king of bliss
Now truly well I know by this
My sacrifice accepted is
Before the Lord today.
A flame of fire sent thou hast
From heaven on high into this place.
I thank thee Lord for this thy grace.
And so I shall always.

CAIN:
Out, out! How have I wasted these my goods –
The sight of this has boiled my blood.
A flame of fire from heaven stood
On my brothers offering.

His sacrifice I see God takes,
And mine refuses and forsakes.
My body all for shame shakes,
In envy of this thing.

GOD:

Why are you angry Cain, say why.
Your face changes wondrously.
You must do well and truly
To have reward of me.

But Cain, thou shalt have all thy will,
If your duty you fulfill.
Abel obeys you. Be careful still,
Or evil may you speed.

CAIN:

Ah well, well is it so?
Come with me, we must go
Into the field down there below.
I have something I want to say.

ABEL:

Brother I am ready
To go with you right meekly.
You are older than I.
I will always obey.

CAIN:

Say, you creep you crawler you clown,
Do you think you'll beat me for renown?
Do you think that you can cast me down?
I'll be master if I may.
God has challenged me, warned me here
Because of you, in right foul manner -
And for that you'll play full dear,
Before you go away.

Your gift by God accepted is.
You can tell by the fire which one it is.
Never again will you see such grace.
You shall die this night.
If God stood here, in this place,
And tried to help you in this case,
Still you would die before his face.
Have this. That puts you right.

Cain kills his brother. Music plays. God enters. Adam and Eve re-enter, on another part of the playing space.

GOD:

Cain, where is your brother Abel?

CAIN:

I know not. I cannot tell.
You should know well
My brother is not in my keeping.

GOD:

What have you done, you wicked man?
Your brother's blood calls out upon
Thee, calls for vengeance as fast as it can.

In the earth I hear it crying.

Cursed on the earth Cain thou shall ever be.
For the deed that thou hast done today
The earth shall waste thy work always
For the wickedness you wrought.
Because thou hast done that mischief
All men will look at you with grief
Idle and wandering like a thief,
For ever set at nought.

Cain speaks mournfully

CAIN   Out alas, where can I be?
Sorrow on each side I see.
If from out this land I flee,
Flying from men's company,
Wild beasts will hunt and savage me.
And if I stay full well I see
I must be bound, no longer free -
And all for my folly.

GOD: No Cain, thou shalt not die soon.
A deed of horror thou hast done.
Death to thee would be a boon.
Thy blood for his will I not shed.
I swear, whoever slayeth thee
Punished seven times shall he be.
Pain and woe can thou never flee
So wicked is thy deed.

To thy deed will thou be bound,
Thou and thy children everyone,
To the seventh generation.
Punishment waits for all.
For thou today has done so
That thy seed for thee shall suffer woe.
As long as thou on earth may go,
My vengeance on thee fall.

CAIN: Out, out, alas alas.
I am damned and cast from grace.
Go I then from place to place
And look out for the best.
Well I know, too well I see,
Whatever place my dwelling be
Each man will loath my company.
So shall I never have rest.

Dad and mam, rest you well.
One foul tale I have to tell.
I have killed my brother Abel.
We fought, I took his life.

ADAM: Alas, alas, is Abel dead?
Cain my son, what have you said

Now every joy from me is fled.
Save only Eve, my wife.

EVE:

Alas, so now my son is slain.
Sorrow falls on us again.
Vengeance is our lot, and pain,
Our life all mourning.

CAIN:

Mother and father farewell to ye.
Out of this land now I will flee.
An outlaw always must I be
No toil shall serve, or thrift.
So God has told me.
Never will I thrive near thee.
I go the first way that I see.
I grant you all my gift.

GOBBET:

Now players from the Wirral are come to you
Noah's tale to tell, as well they can do,
With all the beasts that went two by two -
Or as many as we could find.
You'll see an ark that's fit for the Dee,
A rainbow, a dove, and a raven on high -
Listen well to this story,
And keep it well in mind.

PLAY 3

Noah's Flood

CAST: God
           Noah
           Shem
           Cham
           Japhet
           Noah's wife
           Shem's wife
           Cham's wife
           Japhet's wife
           The gossips

God appears in a high place – or, if possible, in the clouds – to speak to Noah and his family.

GOD: I, God, that all this world has wrought
           Heaven and earth and all from nought,
           I see that my people in deed and thought
           Are foully besotted in sin.
           My spirit cannot dwell in man
           When flesh he sets his heart upon.
           Six score years have come and gone
           And I have patient been.

           Man that I made I will destroy,
           With beasts and worms and fowls that fly.
           Life on earth doth me annoy,
           Such folk now live thereon.
           It harms my heart most hurtfully
           The malice that men can multiply.
           It grieves me sore, right inwardly
           That ever I made man.

           Noah, my servant free –
           You are a righteous man I see.
           Make a ship soon, I say to thee.
           Find trees both dry and light.
           Little rooms inside must you make.
           Bind it with cords too hard to break.
           Both inside and outside great care see thou take
           To tar it over with all your might.

           Three hundred cubits it should be long
           And fifty across to make it strong.
           In height, sixty. Don't get it wrong.
           Measure it all about.
           Put in a window, use your wits,
           A cubit in breadth and length make it.

On the side, a door that shuts,
For coming in and out.

Somewhere to eat you should make also,
Chambers with rooves on, one or two,
For I will make the waters flow,
I can unmake and make.
All the world destroyed shall be,
Except for you, your wife and your sons three.
Their wives as well shall go with thee.
All else shall fall, before your face.

NOAH: I thank thee loud, Lord, I thank thee still,
That you show me such high good will,
That me and my household you spare to kill,
As now I truly find.
Your bidding Lord I will fulfill,
Groan or grieve at thee I never will.
Of your grace I have my fill,
Alone of all mankind.

Come on, you men and women all.
Hurry, before the water falls.
Work on the ship, build the chamber and hall,
As God has bid us to.

SHEM: Father, look, I've already found
An axe to use to chop wood down,
As sharp as any in all this town
For the work we've got to do.

CAM: I have a hatchet sharp and keen.
It bites in well, as may be seen.
Its a better ground blade, with an edge more mean
Than any in all this town.

JAPHET: I can make nails and pins,
And use this hammer to knock them in.
Lets get to work and stop this din,
We'll do it, I'll be bound.

NOAH'S WIFE: We can carry the timber too.
There isn't much else we can do.
Women are weak, as well you know,
We can't be at any great trouble.

SHEM'S WIFE: Here's a solid hacking stock.
You can cut on this and knock.
No one's idle in his flock.
We're not that feeble.

CHAM'S WIFE: I will go for tar and sludge
To caulk the ship up and paint it with pitch.
Daubed it must be, every plank and stitch,
Every board stick and pin.

JAPHET'S WIFE: I'll gather twigs and chippings here,
And put them for a fire all together.
I'll find something for dinner
Bt the time you all come in.

Noah begins to build the ark. They work with their different tools.

NOAH: In the name of God I now begin
To make the ship that we sail in.
We must be ready when its time to swim,
At the coming of the flood.
These boards I nail together
Should shelter us from the weather.
We can float along, hither and thither
And stay safe inside from the flood.
From this tree I'll make a mast,
Tied with cables made to last,
With a sail to take each blast.
Each thing's the proper kind.
I've a topcastle and a bowsprit,
The cords and ropes are a perfect fit.
When the flood comes we'll be ready for it.
Our work is at an end.

Wife, in this vessel we must shut up shop.
You and the children, in you hop.

NOAH'S WIFE: In faith, Noah, I wish you'd stop.
You could have a five star hotel in there,
I won't do what you've say.

NOAH: Good wife, now do as I thee bid.

NOAH'S WIFE: By Christ, not I till I see more need.
You can stand all day and stare.

NOAH: Lord, women are crabby, complaining always.
None of them stay quiet, if I dare so say.
Well, you can see it here today,
You're witnesses, everyone.
Good wife, let be with all this stir.
All this fuss you make out here.
They all think you're the master,
And so you are, by St. John.

GOD: Noah, take your family,
Into the ship now hurry ye,
None so righteous seems to me
Of all men living.
Of clean beasts thou should take with thee
Seven pair - count carefully -
Of the others one pair, a he and she.
Two by two they must go in.

All the goods you need, see that you bring,

To sustain the men and beasts therein.
The world is filled full of sin.
It is hateful to my sight.
Forty days and forty nights
Rain shall fall on the foes of right.
That I have made through my own might
Now think I to destroy.

NOAH: Lord to your bidding I am bound.
If no other grace is found
All mankind must now be drowned.
I alone thy favour find.

Have done, men and women all.
Hurry, before the waters fall.
See each beast safe in its stall.
Into the ship let them all be brought.
Of clean beasts there seven should be,
Of unclean two, so God told me.
The flood is coming, as you can see.
Come on now, tarry not.

SHEM: Here are the lions. The leopards are in –
The horses and mares, the oxen and swine,
Goats and calves, cows and kine,
Standing where you can see.

CHAM: Camels and asses we could find,
Buck and doe, hart and hind,
Beasts of every manner and kind
Are coming, it seems to me

JAPHET: Take the dogs, the cats too,
Otters and foxes, badgers also,
Rabbits and hares hopping – off they go –
There's fodder for all to eat.

NOAH'S WIFE: Bears and wolves – all kinds of pets –
Apes and owls and marmosets.
Squirrels, weasels stoats and ferrets,
We must give them all their meat.

SHEM'S WIFE: There's plenty of beasts packed into the house.
One more cat would make it a crowd.
Here a rat and there a mouse
Must stand up close together.

CHAM'S WIFE: Here come the fowl, the big and the small,
The herons and the cranes, the bitterns and daws,
Swans and peacocks, and a good big store
To feed them through this weather.

JAPHET'S WIFE: Here are cocks and kites and crows,
Rooks and ravens, curlews too

Ducks and cuckoos, all the kinds we know,
Each one in its pair.
Here are the doves the sparrows and the drakes,
Plovers from the fields, redshanks from the lakes
Every bird that can sing or shriek
Is safe enough in here.

NOAH: Wife, come in. Why stand out there?
You can be forward enough, I can swear.
Get in - in God's name, its time we were -
If we don't we might well drown.

NOAH'S WIFE: Off you go, set sail at once.
Row forth and good riddance.
I tell you now, there's no chance
Of me going out of town.

My gossips live here, everyone
One foot further will I not be gone.
They won't drown, by St. John,
If I can save their lives.

They love me, they're my mates by Christ.
But you won't let them in your floating chest.
So sail off, Noah, when you think best,
And get yourself a new wife.

NOAH: Shem, son, your mam's in one of her moods.
I've never met such a woman for carrying on so.

SHEM: Don't worry, I'll fetch her in to you.
Have you ever known me fail?
Mother, my father asks you, and so do I,
If you'll get into the ship by and by,
Look up, you can see the sky
We're ready to set sail.

NOAH'S WIFE: Go back to him son and say,
I will not go in there today.

NOAH: Come in wife, you can't stand there all day
By the devil himself, you'll drown if you're out.

CHAM: Shall we fetch her in?

NOAH: Yes son, with Christ's blessing and mine.
We've only got a little time.
The flood comes on, I've got no doubt.

THE GOSSIPS: The flood is flowing with full great haste
On every side it spreads out far.
The fear of drowning fills me fast
Good gossip, let us near.

Let's have a drink before we part,
For many times have we done so.

I've seen you in one draught drink a quart,
And I'll do the same before I go.

Here's a tankard of malmesey good and strong,
It'll warm our hearts and loosen our tongues.
Noah might think we're taking too long,
But we'll drink down every drop.

JAPHET: Mother, we ask you all together,
For here we are, all your children,
Come into the ship for fear of the weather,
For the love of God, have a thought.

NOAH'S WIFE: I won't do that because you call.
I must have my gossips all.

SHEM: No mother, I say you shall,
Whether or not you think you ought.

She goes in

NOAH: Welcome wife, to my little boat.

NOAH'S WIFE: And you can have that.
That will change your note.

She hits him

NOAH: Aha, by heaven, this is much too hot.
It is good to be quiet and still.
Children, I think the boat has moved.
Now all the world is one great flood.
Ah great God, that art so good,
May all work by thy will.

Noah opens the window, and they sing.

The window I will shut anon,
And into my chamber soon begone
Until the weather all is done
And the flood gone by God's might.

Noah shuts the window. There is silence for a little while. Then he opens it again.

NOAH: Now forty days are fully gone,
A raven will I send anon,
To see if earth or tree or stone
Is dry in any place.
And if it come not back again,
It is a sign, sooth to say,
That it is dry on hill or plain,
And God has shown his grace.

He sends out a raven. He takes a dove in his hands.

> Ah Lord, wherever this raven be
> Somewhere is dry, so I see,
> But a dove, will return to me
> So meek you are, so tame.

He sends a dove. It comes back with an olive branch in its beak and gives it into Noah's hands.

> Blessed, Lord, be thou always,
> My sweet dove bears olive, from some dry place.
> It is a token that thou hath sent us grace.
> It is a sign of peace.
> But yet, till thou command me
> I will not leave here hastily.
> Then will I devoutly
> Do thee sacrifice.

GOD:
> Noah, take thy wife anon
> And thy children, everyone,
> And all of ye out of the ship begone,
> All of them with ye.
> The beasts and all the birds that fly,
> They too must go hence by and by
> On earth to grow and multiply.
> It is my will that it is so.
>
> You too shall grow and multiply.
> Rebuild the earth with buildings high.
> Each beast that walks, each bird that flies,
> Shall be afraid of you.
> The fish in the sea shall be your food.
> All trees and roots that shall seem good,
> All beasts that are clean in flesh and blood,
> All shall sustain you.

[God makes a rainbow appear]

> My rainbow stands, between you and me
> There in the firmament it shall be,
> A truthful token for you to see,
> That my vengeance now has ceased.
> Man and woman nevermore
> Will be wasted by water, as they have before.
> Only for sin that grieves me sore
> This my vengeance was.

NOAH:
> Lord God in majesty,
> Such grace have you granted me
> Where all else drowned, safe to be.
> To thy love am I bound.
>
> My wife, my children, my family
> With sacrifice will honour thee.

By the rainbow all can see
The grace that we have found.

GOBBET:

You have seen Noah already today,
With all his company - a fine display.
Now the city's own actors, the Gateway,
Are come before you here.
They tell the story of Abraham,
To God the most beloved of men,
And how one day, God commanded him
To kill his son most dear.

PLAY 4

Abraham and Isaac

CAST:　　　　　　　**God**
　　　　　　　　　Abraham
　　　　　　　　　Isaac
　　　　　　　　　Narrator ('Gobbet on the Green')
　　　　　　　　　Angel [here, Gobbet]

ABRAHAM:　　　Ah, thou high God, granter of grace,
　　　　　　　　That no end nor beginning has,
　　　　　　　　I thank thee lord, that ever was
　　　　　　　　My help and hope of victory.

God appears to Abraham

GOD:　　　　　　Abraham my servant, I say to thee,
　　　　　　　　Thy help and thy succour I will be.
　　　　　　　　For thy good deeds much pleaseth me,
　　　　　　　　I tell thee truthfully.

Abraham turns to God

ABRAHAM:　　　Lord, one thing I wish to see,
　　　　　　　　That I pray for with heart full free.
　　　　　　　　Grant me, through thy majesty,
　　　　　　　　Some fruit of my body.

　　　　　　　　I have no child, foul or fair.
　　　　　　　　Some other's child must be my heir.
　　　　　　　　That fills my heart with heavy care.
　　　　　　　　On me, lord, have mercy.

GOD:　　　　　　Nay Abraham, friend, believe thou me,
　　　　　　　　No stranger's child thy heir shall be.
　　　　　　　　But one son I shall send thee,
　　　　　　　　Begotten of thy body.

　　　　　　　　Abraham, do as I thee say.
　　　　　　　　Look up and number, If thou may,
　　　　　　　　The stars that stand in the sky.
　　　　　　　　Not possible, it seems.

　　　　　　　　To so much folk the father shall thou be
　　　　　　　　Kings from thy seed for men to see,
　　　　　　　　And one child, of great degree
　　　　　　　　All mankind shall redeem.

Each man child hence, I thee say,
Shall be circumcised on his eighth day,
And thou thyself full soon.
Who circumcised not is
Then unobedient that man is.
Look that this be done.

ABRAHAM: Blessed be thou ever and aye,
For by this sign then know thou may
Thy folk from other men.

NARRATOR [GOBBET]: You see by this, in the Old Testament
This was sometimes a sacrament.
But when Christ died, away it went,
And baptism came instead.

Gods promise was our prophesy
Of Jesus and Our Lady.
For both came of that family
Where Abraham was head.

GOD: Abraham, my servant, Abraham!

ABRAHAM: Lo Lord, all ready here I am.

GOD: Take Isaac, thy son by name,
That thou lovest the best of all,
And in sacrifice offer him to me
Upon that hill there besides thee.
Abraham, it is my will that so it be,
Whatever may befall.

ABRAHAM: My Lord, it is ever my intent
To thee to be obedient.
That son that thou to me has sent
Offer I will to thee,
And fulfill thy commandment
With heart-felt will and full assent.
High Lord, God omnipotent,
Thy bidding done shall be.
My wife and children every one
Shall stay at home, save Isaac my son
He must with me be gone.

Abraham turns to Isaac

ABRAHAM: Make thee ready, my dear darling,
For we must do a little thing.
This wood do thou on thy back bring.
We may no longer stay.

A sword and fire I will take
For sacrifice that I must make.
Gods bidding will I not forsake,
But ever obedient be.

Abraham takes a sword and fire. Isaac takes a bundle of sticks and goes after his father.

ISAAC:
Father I am ready
True to do your bidding am I,
To bear this wood full meekly
If you command me.

ABRAHAM:
O Isaac, Isaac, my darling dear,
My blessing now I give thee here.
Take up this bundle with good cheer.
And bear it on thy back.

ISAAC:
Father to do your bidding I will never slack.

ABRAHAM:
Now Isaac, son, go we our way
To yonder mount, if that we may.

They both go to the place of sacrifice

ISAAC:
My dear father I will away
And try to follow you.

Abraham, intending to kill his son, lifts his hands to heaven

ABRAHAM:
O, my heart will break in three!
To hear thy words I have pity.
As thou will, lord, so must it be.
To thee I will be true.

Lay down thy bundle, my own son.

ISAAC:
All ready, father. See it done.
But why make you so heavy cheer?
Is there aught for thee to fear?
Father, if it be thy will,
Where is the beast that we shall kill?

ABRAHAM:
There is none, son, upon the hill
I can see none but us two here.

Isaac fears that his father will kill him

ISAAC:
Father I am full sore afraid
To see you bear that drawn sword.
I hope for all of middle earth
You will not slay your child.

Abraham comforts his son

ABRAHAM:
Comfort, child, and do not dread.
Our lord will send of his godhead
Some manner of beast into this field
A tame beast or wild.

ISAAC: Father tell me, or I go,
            Whether I be harmed or no.

ABRAHAM: Ah dear God that I am woe!
            Thou burst my heart in sunder.

ISAAC: Father tell me, in that case,
            Why you your sword drawn in this place.
            Of that I have great wonder.

ABRAHAM: Isaac son, peace I pray thee.
            You break my heart in three.

ISAAC: I pray thee father, keep nothing from me.
            But tell me what you think.

ABRAHAM: Ah, Isaac, Isaac, I must thee kill.

ISAAC: Alas father, is that your will,
            Your own child's blood to spill
            Upon this mountains brink?

            If I have trespassed in any degree
            With a stick you might beat me.
            Put up your sword, if so it will be.
            I am but a child.

ABRAHAM: O my dear son I am sorry
            To do to thee this great annoy.
            God's commandment do must I.
            His works are ever mild.

ISAAC: Would God my mother were here with me.
            She would kneel down upon her knees
            And pray to you, father, if it might be,
            For to save my life.

ABRAHAM: O comely creature, unless I kill
            I grieve my God, and that full ill.
            I may not work against his will
            But ever obedient be.
            O Isaac son, to thee I say,
            God has commanded me this day
            That sacrifice - 'no' I cannot say -
            I make him of thy blood.

ISAAC: Is it God's will I shall be slain?

ABRAHAM: Yea son, and it must be so.
            To his bidding I will be true
            And ever please him.
            Unless I do this doleful deed
            My lord will not help me in my need.

ISAAC:

Nay then father, God forbid
But you make your offering.

Father, at home your sons you find,
Sons you love by course of kind.
Once I am gone out of your mind,
Your sorrows may soon cease.
But you must do God's bidding.

Father, tell my mother for nothing.

Abraham wrings his hands

ABRAHAM:

For sorrow I my hands wring.
Thy mother this will not please.
Oh Isaac, Isaac, blessed may thou be.
My wits I almost lose for thee.
The blood of thy body so free
I cannot bear to shed.

Isaac kneels

ISAAC:

Father since you needs must do so,
Let it pass lightly and let it go.
I kneel upon my knees to you.
May your blessings on me spread.

ABRAHAM:

My blessing, dear son, give I thee
And thy mothers with heart so free.
The blessing of the Trinity
My dear son, light on thee.

ISAAC:

Father I pray you blindfold me
Your stroke, father, I would not see.
I might cry out fearfully
To see the sword so keen.

ABRAHAM:

My dear son Isaac speak no more
Thy words have made my heart full sore.

ISAAC:

Oh dear father, wherefore, wherefore?
Since I must needs be dead
For one thing I will you pray.
Since I must die the death today
Use as few strokes as you may
When you strike off my head.

ABRAHAM:

Your meekness child fills me with fear.
Well may I sing a sad song here.

ISAAC:

O dear father do away, with your despair.
Do not mourn me so.

Now truly father, our talking
Makes for long delaying.

I pray you, now, make ending,
And let me hence be gone.

ABRAHAM: Come hither, my child. Thou art so sweet.
Now must I bind thy hands and feet.

Isaac rises and goes to his father, who takes him and binds him and lays him on the altar for sacrifice.

ISAAC: Father we must no more meet
For aught that I can see.
But do with me then as you will.
We must obey and use our skill
God's commandment to fulfill.
For needs so it must be.

Father, greet well my brethren young,
And pray my mother for her blessing.
I come no more under her wing.
Farewell, forever and aye.

But father, I cry you mercy
For all my trespasses unto thee.
Forgive me father, if it may be,
Unto doomsday.

ABRAHAM: My dear son, let be thy moans.
My child, they grieve me, every one.
Blessed be thou, body and bone,
For I forgive thee here.
Now my dear son, here shall thou lie.
Unto my work now must I fly.
I would it were myself to die,
Not thou, my darling dear.

ISAAC: Father, if you be to me kind,
About my head a kerchief bind,
And let me lightly out of your mind,
As soon as I am sped.

ABRAHAM: Farewell, sweet son of grace.

Abraham kisses Isaac, and binds a cloth around his head.   Isaac kneels.

ISAAC: I pray you father, turn down my face
A little time, while you have space,
For I am full sore adread.

ABRAHAM: To do this deed I am sorry.

ISAAC: Yes Lord, to thee I call and cry.
On my soul have mercy, heartily I thee pray.

ABRAHAM: Lord, I would fain work thy will.
This young innocent that lies so still,

I am full loth for to kill,
By any manner of way.

ISAAC: Ah mercy, father, why tarry you so?
Strike off my head and let me go.
I pray you, rid me of my woe,
For now I take my leave.

ABRAHAM: My son, my heart will break in three
To hear thee speak such words to me.
Jesu, take pity upon me
For thou art all my mind.

ISAAC: Now father, I see that I shall die,
Almighty God in majesty
My soul I offer unto thee.
Lord, to me be kind.

Abraham is about to cut off Isaac's head with the sword, when the angel [here, Gobbet] takes the end of the sword and stops it.

ANGEL [GOBBET] Abraham, my servant dear!

ABRAHAM: Lo, lord, I am all ready here.

ANGEL [GOBBET] Lay not thy sword in no manner
On Isaac, thy dear darling.
Do him no annoy.
God has sent by me this day
A lamb that is both good and gay.
Look, I have him here.

ABRAHAM: Ah Lord of heaven, and king of bliss,
Thy bidding shall be done on this.
A sacrifice here sent me is,
And all, lord, through thy grace.
A horned wether here I see.
Among these briars tied is he.
To thee he offered now shall be,
Right here in this place.

Abraham takes the lamb and kills him

GOD: Abraham, by myself I swear,
Since thou hast been obedient here
And spared not thy son to tear
To fulfill my bidding,
Thou shall be blessed for pleasing me.
Thy seed shall I so multiply
Like stars and sand, so many shall be
Of thy body's breeding.

And of all nations, believe thou me,
Thou blessed ever more shall be
Through the fruit that comes of thee,

A saviour from thy seed.

NARRATOR [GOBBET]: This deed you saw done in this place
In prophesy of Jesus done it was.
He, for to win mankind grace,
Was sacrificed on the cross.

By Abraham we may understand
The father of heaven, who gave his son
Jesus to break the devils bond.
Or else we all were lost.
By Isaac understand we may
Jesus, that was obedient aye
His fathers will to work always
And death for to confound.

He kneels

Such obedience grant us O lord,
Ever to thy most holy word.
Then altogether shall we
That worthy king in heaven see,
And dwell with him in great glory
For ever and ever, Amen.

INTERVAL

———————

GOBBET: From over the Mersey comes the play you'll next see,
The pageant of Mary, of mercy mild Queen,
Of the Roman Octavian, a king cruel and keen,
And of Sybil, the pagan sage.
If you witness well this royal thing
I grant you all the blessing
Of the high imperial king,
Of the emperor and his page.

PLAY 5

The Nativity

CAST:
            Gabriel
            Mary
            Joseph
            Angel [here, role shared with Gobbet]
            Messenger
            Octavian
            Two Senators
            The Sybil
            Two midwives (Tybil and Salome)

GABRIEL:
Hail to thou, Mary, mother free,
Full of grace. God is with thee.
Among all women blessed thou be,
In the fruit of thy body.

MARY:
Ah Lord that sits on high,
At this wonder marvel I.
A simple maid of my degree,
Greeted so graciously.

GABRIEL:
Mary, dread thou nothing in this.
With great God found thou has
Among all others special grace.
Therefore Mary, know thou can

Conceive and bear - I say to thee -
A child. Jesus his name shall be.
So great shall never none be as he.
And called God's son.

MARY:
Thou beast so bright, how may this be?
No man in sin has known me.

GABRIEL:
The Holy Ghost shall light in thee
And shade thee from men's sight.

That holy one, believe thou me,
Shall come from God in majesty
As son of God shall he known be,
All through his father's might.

MARY:
Now since God will that so it be
And such grace hath sent to me,
Blessed evermore be he.
May all be to his liking.

The angel goes

And so 'Magnificat' sing I,
With joyful mirth and melody.
For Christ comes to our kind in me
Of mercy to be king.

Mary sings a magnificat

Much my Lord has done for me
To save all men from shame.
So with a heart right full and free
I magnify his name.

He pushes the mighty from their place
And the mild he makes to rise.
The hungry, needy, wanting grace
With God he satisfies.

Riches and power he forsakes
And to me he enters in.
From woe to joy all men he wakes
To show mercy to man's sin.

JOSEPH: Alas, alas and woe is me!
Who has made her with child?
Three months she hath been gone from me.
Now has she gotten her, hark to me,
A great belly, as I see,
Since she went away.

And mine it is not, be thou bold,
For I am both old and cold;
These thirty winters, though I would,
I could not play no play.

God, never let an old man
Take to wife a young woman
Nor set his heart her upon,
Lest he be beguiled.

For accord there may be none,
They may never be at one.
And that is seen in many a one,
As well as here with me.

I will go from her.
Yet shame her will I nought,
Feebly though my wife has wrought.
To leave her privately is my thought,
So no man knows the case.

So heavy at heart it maketh me
That now to sleep I taketh me.
Lord on her have mercy
For her misdeed today.

ANGEL: Joseph, let be thy feeble thought.
Take Mary thy wife and dread thee nought.
For wickedly she has not wrought,

But this is God's will.

The child that she shall bear, hear this
Of the Holy Ghost begotten is,
To save mankind that did amiss
And prophecy to fulfil.

JOSEPH: Ah now I know lord it is so
I will let no man be her foe,
But while I may on earth go
With her I will be.
Now Christ has come among our kind
As the prophets had divined
Lord God in contented mind
With Joy I worship thee.

[Octavian and his messenger enter on horseback. Joseph and Mary withdraw]

MESSENGER: Make room my lords and give us way
And let Octavian come and play,
And Sybil the sage, that fair faced maid
To tell you a prophesy.

That Lord that died on good Friday
Save you all, both night and day.
Farewell, my lords, I go my way.
I can no longer abide.

OCTAVIAN: I am the prince most of power
Under heaven the highest here.
All this world, without fear,
King, prince, baron, bachelor,
Be ready for me to doom.

My name Octavian called is.
No man on earth dare do amiss
Against me - I tell you this -
Nay, no man can say that aught is his
Unless from me it come.

I have multiplied more
The city of Rome since I was born.
For what with strength and strokes full sore
All this world, under my law,
Pays tribute unto Rome.

Therefore my lords, now likes it me
To prove my might and majesty.
I will send about and see
How many folk I have.

All the world shall written be
Great and small in each degree
That dwell in shire or city -
King, clerk, knight and knave.

Each man one penny shall pay,
Therefore, my beadle, do as I say.

In the middle of the world, by any way,
That game will now begin.

The folks of Judah, in good faith,
At the mid-point live - that is no lie.
So go thou thither, day by day,
And see thou stop not on the way.

Warn him that is there president
That each man must be present
And by that penny, as their rent,
To know to be obedient
To Rome, that makes them thrall.

Warn them boy - I command thee -
In each land shire and city
To do the same. Say this from me.
So all the world shall know that we
Are sovereign over all.

Come on boy! Art thou not gone?

MESSENGER: Thy errand, my lord, shall soon be done.
No raw-arsed ram in all this town
Can go as fast as me.

OCTAVIAN: For that, boy, by my crown,
A ride upon the gallows tree
Is my reward to thee.

MESSENGER: This hackney well will serve me,
For high and swift is he.
For all, gramercy, Lord.

OCTAVIAN: Boy, there are ladies, many a one.
Among them all, chose thee one.
Take the fairest, or else none,
And freely I give her thee.

[The Senators enter]

FIRST SENATOR: My Lord Octavian, we be sent
From all of Rome with good intent
From rich and poor in parliament.
And to this point we all assent -
As God to honour thee.

SECOND SENATOR: Yes truly sir, their will is this -
To honour thee as God with bliss.
No man in thy time lost aught of his.
Peace hath been long and yet is,
In this, thy loyal city.

OCTAVIAN: I thank you my friends, in good faith.
But I must die, I know not what day.
Folly it were in many a way

To desire such dignity.

For all of flesh and blood and bone
Made I am, not iron, tree or stone.
And of my life, most part is gone,
Age shows him so in me.

Godhead hath no beginning,
And never shall have ending.
Though I be highest worldly king,
None of this have I.

But yet enquire of this will we
Of her that hath the grace to see
Things that afterward shall be
By spirit of prophecy.

And after her learning, then work will I,
Discussing all difficulty,
I take no more on me
Than I am full worthy.

Sybil the sage, tell me this thing.
You have wit as no man living.
Shall ever any earthly king
Pass me in degree?

SYBIL: Yes sir, I tell thee without delaying.
A babe shall be born, bliss to bring,
Which never had beginning
Nor ever shall ended be.

OCTAVIAN: Sybil, I pray especially,
By sign that thou would certify
What time that lord so royally
His kingdom shall begin.

The Sybil Speaks

SYBIL: Sir I shall tell you truthfully
His signs when they are clear to me
For when he comes through his mercy
All mankind will he win.

For by my faith I know well this,
That God will bring mankind to bliss
And send from heaven - believe well this -
His son, our saviour.

But what time sir, in good faith,
That he will come I cannot say.
Therefore in this place I will pray
To greatest God of might.

And if to see aught that I may
Ghostly, or by any way
Warn you I shall anon this day,
And show it to your sight.

The Sybil prays.   [Octavian and the senators withdraw. Joseph comes forward.] The messenger speaks in a loud voice.

MESSENGER: Peace I bid, king and knight,
Man and woman here in sight
My Lord Octavian, much of might,
Commands you tribute bring.

He will record each country.
Castle shire and city.
A penny from each man asketh he,
To acknowledge he is king.

JOSEPH: Ah lord, what doth this boaster here?
A poor man's wealth can cost him dear.
Now comes the king's messenger
To see what he can get.

Castle tower and rich manor
I never had in my power.
With axe and nail and hammer
I have won my meat.

The angel told of marvellous things.
He that man from woe shall bring
Is in my good wife's keeping.
That makes me more bold.

Ah, dear sir, tell me I thee pray:
Shall poor as well as rich pay?
My faith sir, I hope nay,
That were a wondrous wrong.

MESSENGER: Good man I warn thee in good faith
To Bethlehem to take the way,
In danger you may fall today,
If you wait too long.

JOSEPH: Now since it may not other be
Mary, sister, now go we.
An ox I will take with me
And there he shall be sold.

[Mary, Joseph and the angel set off with the ox and the ass to Bethlehem. They pass two groups of people, one sad, one happy. Joseph goes to look for an inn.]

MARY: Ah lord what may this signify?
Some men I see glad and merry
And some sighing and sorry.
Since Christ is here in me,
All mankind should be glad.

ANGEL [GOBBET]:   God's mother dear, they gladden so
For Christ himself to them will show.
But these shall have no grace to know.
That God for man would stoop so low.

Therefore be they sad.

JOSEPH: Mary, sister, sooth to say
No harbour get we here today.
For great lords in fine array
Occupy this city.

Therefore must we in good faith
Lie in this stable till it be day.
To make men meek he shows the way.
Born here will he be.

MARY: Help me down, my husband dear,
For I feel my time is near.
In this stable that is here
I hope Christ born will be.

JOSEPH: Come to me my darling sweet.
The treasure of heaven in thee I greet.
In full meek manner must I meet
Him that I hope to see.

Mary takes her place [in the stable] between the ox and the ass

Mary sister, I will away
To get two midwives if I may
To tend thee as is this city's way.
I come again full soon.

JOSEPH: **(to the midwives)** Women, God you save and see!
Is it your will to go with me?
My wife is come unto this city
With child. Her time is near.

Help her now, for charity
And stay with her till daylight be.
For your trouble, I say to thee,
I shall pay you right here.

TYBIL: All ready good man, in good faith.
We will do all that ever we may.
For two such midwives, I dare well say,
You'll not find in this city.

SALOME: Come good man, lead us away.
By God's held thy wife shall say
We know our work. Before it's day
Thyself shall well it see.

JOSEPH: Lo Mary, heart, I have brought here
Two midwives, that it may appear
They ease thy pain, my darling dear,
And rest with thee till day.

MARY: Sir, they be full welcome here.
                        But God will work his power
                        Right soon for me, my husband dear,
                        For he is best, now and for aye.

There is a short silence.   [Mary gives birth to Jesus.]

MARY: Ah, Joseph, tidings of joy.
                        I have a son, a sweet boy.
                        Lord God, proven is thy might.

                        Pain felt I none this night.
                        As first into my womb he light,
                        So now he cometh to our sight.

The star appears. Sybil goes to Octavian

SYBIL: Sir Emperor, God thee save and see.
                        I tell you true that born is he.
                        Surpassing all kings, even thee,
                        That are or ever were.

OCTAVIAN: Ah Sybil, this is a wondrous sight,
                        For yonder I see a maiden bright,
                        A young child in her arms held tight,
                        A bright cross on his head.

                        Incense I command thee bring,
                        To honour this child, of mercy king.
                        Should I be God? Nay, such a thing
                        Great wrong in truth it were.

                        For this child is more worthy
                        Than a thousand such as I
                        I am his subject now I see.
                        This child I worship here.

The angel sings

                        Ah Sybil, hears not thou this song?
                        My body all it goes along
                        Joy and bliss makes my heart strong
                        To hear this melody.

                        Sir senators, go home anon
                        And warn my men every one
                        That such worship must not be done
                        As they would do to me.

FIRST SENATOR   Ah Lord, whatever this may be,
                        It is a wondrous sight to see.
                        For in the star, it seems to me,
                        I see a full fair maid.

SECOND SENATOR: Sir, shall this child pass thee
                        In worthiness and dignity?

Such a lord, by my loyalty
I never thought would be.

JOSEPH: Lord welcome, sweet Jesu.
Thy had thy name before I thee knew.
I know now the angel's word is true,
That thou art a clean maid.

For he has come mans bliss to brew
For all that trust in thee will show.
Now man's joy begins anew;
His woe doth pass away.

MARY: Lord, blessed may thou be,
That born so simple art, I see.
To end the devil's mastery
Art thou come today.

Fine linen clothes are not for thee.
Therefore thy sweet body free
In this crib lies joyfully.

TYBIL: Ah dear lord, heaven's king,
That this is a marvellous thing -
No labour pains nor groaning,
And yet she has a son.

I dare well say, believe thou this,
That virgin clean this woman is,
For she has borne a child in bliss,
I've known no other one.

SALOME: Be quiet, Tybil, I thee pray,
For that is false, in good faith.
There was never a woman was clean maid
And with child without a man.

Never you mind, right soon we'll say
Whether that one is clean maid.
I'll know it if I can.

**Salome tries to touch Mary's private parts, but suddenly her hands wither.
She cries out**

Alas, alas, alas.
An evil thing befallen has.
My hands are dried up in this place,
And feeling none have I.

Punishment is now my plight,
For I would tempt God's might.
Alas that I came here this night,
To suffer such annoy.

The star appears, and an angel enters

ANGEL: Woman, beseech this child of grace,
                  That he forgive you your trespass.
                  And before you go out of this place,
                  Mended you may be.

                  This miracle that you see here,
                  Is of God's own power,
                  To bring mankind from danger,
                  And save them, believe you me.

SALOME: Ah, sweet child, I ask mercy
                  For thy mother's love, Mary.
                  Though I have done wretchedly,
                  Sweet child, forgive it me.

Her hands heal

                  Ah blessed be God. All whole am I.
                  Now I believe and truthfully
                  That God is come in mercy.
                  And thou lord, thou art he.

                  ———————

GOBBET: So the infant in his might cast down
                  The royalty of those who once ruled this town.
                  Mighty Caesar must yield his crown
                  To a poor and helpless child.
                  The actors of Clwyd have come together
                  And taken on them, with right good cheer,
                  That the shepherds and their play should now appear,
                  All the way from Wales so wild.

PLAY 6
The Shepherds

CAST: **Hankyn (first shepherd)**
                    Harvey (second shepherd)
                    Tudd (third shepherd)
                    Trowle (the boy)
                    Four boys
                    Angel
                    Joseph
                    Mary

FIRST SHEPHERD: Over the wolds have I walked so wide,
                        Under the bushes my billet I build,
                        From the stiff storms my sheep to shield,
                        My wandering ewes to save.
                        From comely Conway up to Clyde
                        In the shadow of the hills my flock I hide.
                        A better shepherd on the mountain side
                        No earthly man may have.

                        With walking am I weary wrought.
                        In mud and sludge my sheep I sought.
                        My nimble rams are my chief thought,
                        To help them and to heal.
                        The sharp scab on them I sought,
                        Or the rot, to see what that had wrought,
                        Or if the cough had caught -
                        I can cure them of all their ills.
                        Here are my herbs, all safe and sound -
                        Henbane and whorehound,
                        Ribwort, radish and egremond,
                        Laid out in a row.

                        Here is tar, in a pot
                        To heal them from the rot.
                        I can clean them, if I see a spot,
                        And take their tallow, too.

He sits down [on a hill]

                        But no fellowship here have I,
                        But myself alone, in good faith.
                        After them soon will I cry.
                        I'll drink first, if I may.

He drinks

                        How, Harvey, how!

Drive thy sheep down below.
He will not hear unless I blow
With all my health and strength.

He blows his horn

SECOND SHEPHERD: Fellow, now we be well met!
I think one more is needed.
If Tudd was here and with us sat,
Then we might sit and feed us.

They sit

FIRST SHEPHERD   Yes, let's all feed friendly, in faith,
I am at your service.
Cry out loud now, by the day.
Tudd is deaf, he may not hear us.

Second shepherd calls, in a low voice

SECOND SHEPHERD: How now, Tudd, come by thy father's kin.

FIRST SHEPHERD: Call him Tudd, Tibby's son,
Then the shrew will come.
He'll answer to his mam's name.

SECOND SHEPHERD: Come on Tudd, Tibby's son.

THIRD SHEPHERD: Sir, in faith I come.
But I have not done
All I have to do.
I've been boiling a salve for the sheep
And before my wife spots it
With gravel and grit
I'm scouring out her old pan.

Hemlock and goosegrass
With tar from the tarbox must be tamed.
Pennygrass and butter for the fat sheep -
Of this salve I'm not ashamed.

No one should be ashamed to show
The points belonging to their craft.
No one better - as well I know -
In the whole of this land is there left.

And, good men, it is not unknown,
To all those husbands here abouts,
That every man must bow down to his wife -
Commonly for fear of a clout.

Hanekyn, hold up thy hand and have me,
So I am on high there be thee.

FIRST SHEPHERD: Gladly sir. If you want to sit by me.
I'd be loth to deny thee.

SECOND SHEPHERD: Now, since God has gathered us together
With a good heart I thank him for his grace.
Welcome be thou, well fare the weather!
Tudd, will you feed your face?

THIRD SHEPHERD: Lay it out, bring out each
What he has for his supper.
Meat and drink will comfort much
For all men hold them dear.

SECOND SHEPHERD: Here's this day's bread, and bacon,
Onion, garlic, and leeks,
Butter, bought in Blacon,
And fat cheese to grease your cheeks.

THIRD SHEPHERD: Ale from Halton I have,
And hot meat I had for my hire.
A pudding that no man can dispraise,
And oatcakes, from Lancashire.

Look - a sheep's head soused in ale,
A loaf of grain to lay on the green,
And sour milk. My wife has ordained
A noble supper, as can be well seen.

FIRST SHEPHERD: What's to be seen, now shall you see.
I have something in my pack.
A pig's foot and a chitterling, that boiled shall be,
And a haggis at the bottom of my sack.

THIRD SHEPHERD: Stay around, fellows, and you shall see
Hot meat - we serve it here -
Gammon, and other good meat together,
And a pudding with a prick in the end.

FIRST SHEPHERD: My satchel to shake out
To shepherds am I not ashamed
This bit of tongue, peeled round about,
With my teeth shall be trimmed.

They eat together

FIRST SHEPHERD: Go, eat your fill and so will I
For by God, here is good pasture!
Come eat with us, God of heaven high:
But mind, we have no shelter.

SECOND SHEPHERD: Shelter enough we have here,
While that we have heaven over our heads.
Now to wet out mouths time were:
To take this flagon, as you've said.

THIRD SHEPHERD: And this bottle now will I take
For here is the best of ale.
Men live for this liquor's sake.
This game will nowhere fail.

FIRST SHEPHERD: Fellows, now our bellies are full,
Let's think of the boy who looks after the flocks.
Blow your horn and call for Trowle,
Call him up to share some of our stock.

SECOND SHEPHERD: That's well said, Hankyn, in truth.
For us I suppose he seeks.
I'll hold the horn up to my mouth
Till the lad has some of our leeks.

THIRD SHEPHERD: I'll take my horn and make a 'hoo'
That he and all heaven will hear.

They blow   [their horns. Trowle enters, at some distance.]

TROWLE: Good my lord, look on me,
And my flock, where they feed.
Out on the wold walk we.
There are no men here that I can see.

All is plain, all empty.
So come on sheep, on we go.
There's no better than these,
No beast so good of blood and bone.

There's nothing at night or day
That I need and I don't have.
A tar-box and boiling pan,
To make up herbs and salves.

Nettle, hemlock and butter, all that.
And my good dog Dottynoll.
That doesn't care what he barks at.
If any man come by,

And wants to know which way is best,
I'll lift my leg up where I lie
And wish him on his way, go east or west.
Once I lie down, I'll not rise.

A waste of time, that were.
For King or Duke, I'll not get up.
Down I'll sit and take my rest right here,
And pour down this pot like a pope.

That lot, I set at little.
Nay then lads, I set nought by thee.
Filth like you get nothing of my bottle.
Flee if you may, I defy ye.

FIRST SHEPHERD: Trowle, attend to my talking
Get your teeth around this and get chewing.

While you and your sheep have been walking
On this loin we've had good feeding.

TROWLE: Fie on your loin and your sausage and cheese,
Your livers your lights and your lungs,
Your sausages, your sauce and your savouries,
Your sitting without any songs.

I'll keep myself on this hill here.
No hankering after hot meat have I.
I'll leave you fellows together
And watch over your sheep nearby.

SECOND SHEPHERD: Good knave, see you keep
Looking after our sheep,
You won't get any sleep -
So have some of this sauce.

TROWLE: No, the dirt is too deep,
The way too steep.
The grubs all creep
Where you keep house.

So your meat - if I may -
That you offer today
I'll share by no way,
Till I have my wages.

I'd like to dress all fine and gay -
But see the rags, of my array.
Penny-pinching is your pay
To any poor page.

THIRD SHEPHERD: Trowle boy, for God's pity,
Come and eat a morsel with me.
Then wrestle will we,
Here on the wold.

TROWLE: That's a sport that's dear to me.
Though I wrestle with all three,
By my high heraldry
My ground I'll hold.

Trowle goes over to his masters.

TROWLE: Here he comes, Trowle the true -
Standing straight and standing right
To fight his masters. I challenge you -
Come on. Who has most might?

FIRST SHEPHERD: Trowle, better food you never knew.
Eat of this - meat for a knight.

TROWLE: No, spare it. If I spew
I hope I chuck it all on you.

SECOND SHEPHERD: This lad longs to be lame,
To lose a limb must be his aim.

TROWLE: Have done. Let's start the game.
Watch out that your bollocks don't break
That wouldn't please your old dame,
A bath in the Dee you're heading to take.

FIRST SHEPHERD: False lad, fie on your face.
On this ground you'll have a fall.

TROWLE: Hankyn, Shepherd, shame thee I shall.
You'll be the worse, you'll be weaker than you were.

He throws the first shepherd.

SECOND SHEPHERD: Boy, before I break your bones,
Kneel down and ask me a boon.

He throws the second shepherd.

TROWLE: Good luck to thee for thy growls and groans.
You'd better hang up your old rags son.

THIRD SHEPHERD: Out alas, he lies, by his loins.
But let me get at that lad.

TROWLE: Watch your arses and watch your groins -
I'll hold on to the luck that I have had.
I'll mangle you more
Than I did before
To this braggart.
Yes, even more.
So keep to the score
For fear of a fart.

He throws the third shepherd.

TROWLE: Lie there, lively in the lake.
All my winnings now I'll snatch -
The cups, the cat's meat and the cake,
I've cast you down, so this is my catch.
May the devil come you three to take,
For traitors, a treacherous batch.
Over the wold with this will I walk,
And everyone will wonder at me as they watch.

Trowle withdraws.

FIRST SHEPHERD: I will wait here on the wold
For I am weary.

SECOND SHEPHERD: If we're weary it's no wonder,
What between wrestling and waking.

THIRD SHEPHERD: We may often be over, though now we be under.
God amend it with his making.

They sit down. The star appears.

FIRST SHEPHERD: What is all this light here
That blazes so bright here
On my black beard.
A man might have a fright here
To see this light here,
For I am afeard.

TROWLE: That star, if it stand,
Will I seek over land,
Though my sight fail me.

He looks up at the sky.

Ah, by God's might!
In yonder star there is light.
From the sun comes this sight
Or so it seems.

SECOND SHEPHERD: Fellows, should we
Kneel down on our knees,
For comfort.
So the true trinity
Will lead us to see
Our lord.

TROWLE: Lord, for this light
Send us some sight
Of why it was sent.
Before this night
I never had such fright
Of the firmament.

THIRD SHEPHERD: Nor I. By my faith,
It is now like day;
So was it never.
So I pray -
Tell the truth to us, say,
To the three of us together.

The angels sing 'Gloria in excelsis deo et in terra pax hominibus bonae voluntatis'.

FIRST SHEPHERD: Fellows, listen there.
Can you not hear
The music on high.

SECOND SHEPHERD: In 'glore' and in 'glere'?
But there was nobody near,
Not to my sight.

THIRD SHEPHERD: Nay, it was 'glory'.
Now I am sorry
There wasn't more song.

TROWLE: This is a strange story.
Such mirth is merry.
I hope it lasts long.

THIRD SHEPHERD: What song was it, say ye,
That he sang to us three?
Expounded it shall be,
Before we pass.
I am the eldest of degree,
And also the best, as it seems to me.
It was 'glorus glorus' with a bit of 'glee'.
That was it, neither more nor less.

TROWLE: No. It was 'glorus glarus glorius'.
That was the note that went over the house.
He was a goodlooking man, and curious,
But away soon he was.

FIRST SHEPHERD: Nay, it was 'glorus glarus' with a 'glo',
And a lot of 'celsis' too.
And as ever I have rest from woe,
He said something about 'glass'.

SECOND SHEPHERD: There wasn't any glass or gly.
Come on fellows, have another try.

THIRD SHEPHERD: By my faith, he was some spy,
Our sheep to steal.
Or he was a man of our own craft.
He was seemly, and wondrous deft.

TROWLE: Nay - he came by night - while all was left -
To put his mark on our ram's tails.

FIRST SHEPHERD: Nay, by God, it was a 'gloria'.
An angel spoke when they sang so.
He had a much better voice than I have,
In heaven they all are so.

SECOND SHEPHERD: Did you hear how he sang 'celsis',
How sadly on that note he set him?
He neither sang of 'sar' nor 'cis'
Nor 'pax merry Maud when she met him'.

THIRD SHEPHERD: And after pax or peace,
Up like a magpie he piped.
Such a melody - and it was no less -
I never in my life so much liked.

TROWLE: And yet, and yet, he sang more too.
                   From my mind it shall not start.
                   He sang also of a 'Deo'.
                   I thought that healed my heart.

FIRST SHEPHERD: Now pray we to God with good intent,
                   Sing I will, and his word embrace.
                   To their song I assent.
                   Let him send us of his grace.

TROWLE: Sing on. Let's see.
                   I will start the song, if I may.
                   All men here sing after me.
                   Listen and you'll learn a song today.

They sing 'troly loly loly lo'. The four boys that have looked after the sheep come forward.

SECOND SHEPHERD: Now follow we the star that shines
                   Till we come to the holy stable.
                   To Bethlehem we bend our limbs
                   To find the fact, not fable.

They go to Bethlehem.

THIRD SHEPHERD: Wait now, no more steps,
                   For now the star begins to stand.
                   Harvey, we are in luck perhaps.
                   I think our saviour is found.

The angel appears.

ANGEL: Shepherds, at this sight
                   Have no fright.
                   This is God's might.
                   Bear that in mind.
                   To Bethlehem go as is right.
                   There you shall see in sight
                   That Jesus is born tonight
                   To recover all mankind.

TROWLE: To Bethlehem we take the way,
                   For with you I think I'll go.
                   To the prince of peace will I pray,
                   So I might heaven know.

                   Sing we all, I say,
                   Make mirth for his majesty,
                   For see it certainly we may,
                   The son of heaven's king is he.

FIRST SHEPHERD: See, see, surely
                   I see Mary.
                   And Jesus Christ just by,
                   Lapped in hay.

TROWLE: Peace, now I see this,
                  In my breast builds bliss.
                  Never again will I do amiss,
                  For that to him hateful is.

SECOND SHEPHERD: Whatever old man is this?
                  Take heed how his head is white and hoar.
                  His beard is a brush of briars,
                  There's a pound of hair around his mouth and more.

THIRD SHEPHERD: It's more of a marvel to me now
                  How much of a nap he needs.
                  His heart must be worn out now,
                  Of his health he must take heed.

FIRST SHEPHERD: Well, what if his beard be rough,
                  Right well to her wants he heeds.
                  Worthy sir, we would like to know now
                  Will you teach us right worthily.

MARY: Shepherds, truly I see,
                  That my son sent you here
                  Through God's might and majesty
                  That shone in me, a maiden clear.

JOSEPH: Go ye forth, and preach this thing.
                  Go altogether on your way.
                  Say you have seen the heaven's king,
                  Come all mankind to save.

FIRST SHEPHERD: Great God, sitting on thy throne,
                  That made all things of nought,
                  Now we thank thee, each one.
                  This is he that we have sought.

SECOND SHEPHERD: Go we up to him anon,
                  With such as we have brought -
                  No ring, or brooch, or precious stone.
                  Let's see what we can offer.

THIRD SHEPHERD: Let us do him homage.

FIRST SHEPHERD: Who shall go first, the page?

SECOND SHEPHERD: No, you are the father in age.
                  So you must first offer.

FIRST SHEPHERD: Hail, king of heaven so high,
                  Born in a crib.
                  Mankind, unto thee,
                  Thou hast made thy kin.

                  Hail king, born in a maiden's bower.
                  Prophets did tell thou shouldst be our saviour.
                  So scholars say.

Look. I bring you a bell.
I pray you, save me from hell,
So I may with thee dwell,
And serve thee, for aye.

SECOND SHEPHERD: Hail, the emperor of hell
And heaven also.
The fiend shall thou fell,
That hath ever been false.

Hail, the maker of the star
That stood us before.
Hail, the most blessed baron
That ever was born.
Look son, I bring thee a flagon,
Look, there hangs a spoon,
For you to eat your porridge with at noon,
As I have often done.
With all my heart, I pray thee, take it.

THIRD SHEPHERD: Hail, prince without a peer,
That mankind shall relieve.
Hail enemy to Lucifer,
Who beguiled Eve.

Hail, the granter of hope,
Now that on earth thou dwells.
Look son, I bring thee a cap,
For I have nothing else.

The gift, son, that I give is small,
And though I come the last of all,
When thou men to bliss call,
Good lord, think on me.

TROWLE: Lord, with all duty I thee address
With the ceremony due to my status.
And to save me from all sickness
I offer thee a pair of my wife's old hose.

For other jewels, my son,
I have none to give
That is worth anything at all,
But for my good heart while I live,
And my prayers till death doth call.

FIRST BOY: Now to you, my fellows, this I do say,
Here in this place before we go away
To that child over there let us go pray,
As our masters have done before

SECOND BOY: Such goods as we have here,
Let us offer them to this prince so dear,
And to his mother, that maiden clear,
That of her body has him borne.

FIRST BOY: Wait sirs, I will go first to the king.

SECOND BOY: I will go next to where he is sitting.

THIRD BOY: Then I will be last in the offering.
That's all, I can say no more.

FIRST BOY: Now Lord, to give thee I have nothing,
No gold or silver, no brooch or ring,
And no rich robes fit for a king.
I have none of that in store.

But, though it lack its stopple,
You can have this, my best bottle.
It will hold a good tipple.
In faith, I can give the no more.

SECOND BOY: Lord, I know that thou art of this virgin born,
In a full poor state sitting there on her arm.
To bow down to thee have I no scorn,
Though thou be but a little child.

I have no jewel to give thee
To maintain thy royal dignity.
But here's my hood - take it thee,
As thou art God and man.

THIRD BOY: Oh noble child of thy father on high,
Alas, what have I to give to thee?
Only my pipe, that sounds so royally.
Truly, I have nothing else at all.
Were I on the rocks or in the valley below,
I could make this pipe sound out so loud,
That all the world should ring,
And tremble as if it would fall.

FOURTH BOY: Now child, although you've come from God,
And be God thyself in thy manhood,
I know that in your childhood
For sweet things thou wilt look.
Poor old Joseph will hurt his thumbs
To pull you down apples pears and plums.
You look as if you need to find more crumbs,
So I give you my nut-hook.

FIRST SHEPHERD: Now farewell, mother and maid,
For of sin thou nothing knowest.
Thou hast brought forth this day
God's son, of might the most.

SECOND SHEPHERD: Brothers, let us all three
Singing walk homewards.
Unkind will I never in no case be.
I will preach all that I know
As Gabriel, by his grace, taught me.

THIRD SHEPHERD: Over the sea, if I have the grace
                    Will I journey now,
                    To preach this thing in every place.
                    Sheep no more will I keep now.

TROWLE: I think we should agree
                    For our misdeeds amends to make,
                    For so now will I.
                    And to the child I wholly me betake,
                    For ever, truly.
                    Shepherd's craft I forsake.
                    As a holy man hereby
                    I will in my prayers watch and wake.

FIRST SHEPHERD: And I a hermit,
                    To praise God, to pray
                    To go by field and sty,
                    To walk in the wilderness always.
                    No man will I meet
                    But my living of him will I pray,
                    No shoes on my feet,
                    And thus will I live for ever and aye.

                    For aye, for ever and for always
                    This world I fully refuse
                    In youth we have been fellows.
                    Friendly let us kiss.

SECOND SHEPHERD: From London to Louth
                    I know not where such a shepherd is.
                    Go you north or south,
                    God grant you all his bliss.

THIRD SHEPHERD: To that bliss may great God bring you,
                    If his will it be.
                    Amen, sing you.
                    Good men, farewell ye.

TROWLE: May all be well, each friend.
                    May God of his might so grant you.
                    For here and now we make an end.
                    Farewell, for we go from you.

GOBBET: To the Makeshift Mummers it doth befall
                    To bring out before us three Kings royal,
                    Who stride into mighty Herod's hall,
                    Tidings of Christ to hear.
                    But Herod, King of Galilee,
                    Swore that he would Christ destroy.
                    He slew all innocents, in his cruelty,
                    All younger than two years.

PLAY 7
Magi and Innocents

CAST: Three kings (Jaspar, Balthazar, Melchior)
Angel [here, role shared with Gobbet]
Messenger
Herod
Doctor
Mary
Joseph
Herod's Messenger
Two solders (Sir Grimball and Sir Waradrake)
Two women
A devil

The three Magi enter and go up to a mountain to pray

FIRST KING: Lord, such time as is thy will
Ancient prophecy to fulfill,
Give us grace, speak loud or still.
By some sign thy coming show.

SECOND KING: Yes Lord, though we are unworthy,
On us, your men, have mercy.
The day of thy birth, pray certify
Here to thy knights three.

THIRD KING: Lord, God, leader of Israel,
Thou would die for thy people's health.
Come now, do not thyself conceal,
But be our counsellor.

The star appears

ANGEL: Rise up, ye kings three,
And come along after me,
Into the land of Judee,
As fast as ever you may.
The child you seek there shall you see
Born all of a maiden free,
That king of heaven and earth shall be
And all mankind shall save.

The kings get up

FIRST KING: Well sirs, my advice to everyone
- find dromedaries to ride upon.
For swifter beasts be there none.

One I have, as you see.

They get on their camels and ride about

SECOND KING: Alas, where has the star gone?
Light to see by is there none.
I know not now what path we're on,
Or which way we should take.

THIRD KING: It is good that we enquire
If anyone can help us here.
Say, officer, that rides by there,
Tell us some tidings.

MESSENGER: Tell me your will, Sir.

FIRST KING: Can you say what place or where
A child is born who the crown will bear,
And of the Jews be king?

SECOND KING: We saw the star shine bright
In the east, a noble sight,
And so we came this way tonight,
With joy to worship him.

MESSENGER: Hold your peace sir, I you pray.
If King Herod heard you so say,
He would go right mad, by my faith
And fly out of his skin.

THIRD KING: Well, since there is a king so near,
Go we to him in the proper manner.

MESSENGER: You can see his palace well from here,
For therein does he dwell.
But if he knew what you say here -
That one is born with greater power -
You bring yourselves in great danger,
Such a thing to him to tell.

The messenger goes to the king. Minstrels play.

MESSENGER: O noble king and worthy conqueror,
Crowned in gold, sitting on high,
Mahomet save thee, great in honour.

License I require to speak to thee.
Tidings my lord I shall you tell,
That these three kings have told to me.
Where they come from I know not well.
Yonder they stand, as you may see.

FIRST KING: Sire roi, royal et reverent,
Dieu vous garde, omnipotent.

SECOND KING: Nous sommes venus, tout le monde,
Nouvelles pour enquirer.

HEROD: Bien venue, rois gentils
Dites-moi tout votre intent.

THIRD KING: Infant querons nous de grand parent,
Le roi de ciel et terre.

HEROD: Sirs, be careful what you say.
Such tidings make my heart to fail.
I warn you, take back your words again,
For fear of villainy.
There is none so great dares me gainsay
To take my realm and to attain
My power, but he shall have pain
And punishment promptly.

I am king of kings. None is so keen.
I sovereign sire, as all have seen.
I take and tear down in tyranny
Castle tower and town.

I rule the wide world worthily.
I beat all that unobedient be.
I drive the devils doughtily
Deep into hell-dark down.

For I am king of all mankind.
I bid, I beat, I loose, I bind.
I master the moon. Bear this in mind.
That I am most of might.

If you obey not, I you will be beat.
No man will come your wounds to treat.
Look at my anger, look how I sweat.
My heart is not at ease.

Herod draws his sword

All men may know and see
That I am king of Galilee,
Whatsoever he says or does.

What the devil should he be?
A boy, a groom of low degree,
To master all my majesty,
Who rules and reigns so royally,
To make me but a goose.

FIRST KING: Sir, we saw the star appear,
In the east, wondrous clear.

SECOND KING: But when it came to your land here
It vanished clean away.

THIRD KING: Well we know by prophecy
                 That a child born should be
                 To rule the people of Judee.
                 That was said for many a year.

HEROD: That is false, I defy thee.
                 For, in despite of all you three
                 This realm moves all through me.
                 There shall be no other kings here.

                 But now you speak of prophecy
                 I shall find out shortly
                 If you tell the truth or lie.
                 My clerk soon shall see.
                 Doctor, my chief of clergy,
                 Look up in the books of prophecy
                 Of Daniel David and Isai
                 And what thou see there say to me.

                 These kings have come a long way
                 To seek a child - or so they say -
                 That should be born in this country
                 My kingdom to destroy.
                 Seek in each leaf, I thee pray,
                 And what thou finds out in good faith
                 Tell us now here. A bet I lay
                 That these lords lie.

DOCTOR: The holy scripture makes declaration
                 Through the patriarchs and prophets of Christ's nativity
                 When Jacob prophesied by plain demonstration
                 And said that the realm of Judah and its royalty
                 From that family would never taken be
                 Till he were come that most mighty is,
                 Sent from the father, the king of bliss.
                 And now fulfilled is Jacob's prophecy.
                 King Herod, that is now reigning
                 Is no jew born, nor of that progeny,
                 But a stranger, by the romans made their king.
                 The jews know of none from their blood descending
                 To succeed to the sceptre and sovereignty.
                 So Christ is now born our king and Messiah.

HEROD: That is false, by Mahomet full of might.
                 That old villain Jacob, dotty with age
                 Shall hold back by no prophecy the title and right
                 Of the Roman's high conquest, which to me as my heritage
                 Is fallen forever, as a prince of high parentage.
                 If any other king or Messiah to my rule would put stop
                 His head from his body with this sword shall I chop.
                 Read on!

DOCTOR: Esau, to whom the spirit of prophecy
                 Was singularly given through the Holy Ghost
                 In his time prophesied that kings certainly

And folk of strange nations and distant coasts,
That prince's birth to magnify, the prince of might the most,
Should walk in great light, and brightness should appear,
As it did unto these kings in a bright star shining clear.

HEROD: Alas, what presumption should move that peevish page,
Or any elvish godling, to take from me my crown.

Throws down his sword

But by Mahomet, that boy for his great outrage
Shall die under my hand. All of his kin I shall slay and beat
    down.
Such vengeance and cruelty have never been seen.
I shall hack at that harlot with my bright brand so keen,
And smash him to pieces small. Look again,
See if these kings shall find him, and his presence attain.

DOCTOR: David, of all prophets most prepotent,
Prophecied that kings of Tharsis and Araby
With mystical gifts shall come, to present
To that lord and prince, that king and high Messiah.

My lord, by prophecy is proved you before
That in Bethlehem there shall be born
A child to save what were else forlorn,
And rule all Israel.

Herod breaks his sword

HEROD: By cock's soul thou art foresworn.
Have done. Those books shall be ripped and torn.
No king shall wear great Herod's crown.
I will my power wield.
Whatever says David - some shepherd with a sling -
Esau and Jeremy and all their offspring,
There shall be no other Messiah or king,
From my right title me to expel.

But go you forth, you kings three
And enquire if it so be.
But remember, come again to me,
For you I mean to feed.
If he be of such degree
Him will I honour, as well as ye,
As fitting to his dignity
In word and thought and deed.

FIRST KING: We take our leave sir. Have good day,
Till we come again this way.

SECOND KING: Sir, as soon as ever we may.
What we see, so shall we say.

THIRD KING: And of his riches and his array
               We will tell you in good faith.

After the Kings leave, a boy comes in with a pitcher

HEROD: Farewell lords, be on your way.
               But come back fast again.

               This boy so great doth me annoy
               That I grow dull, and wax clean dry.
               Have done, and fill the wine up high,
               I die without a drink.
               Fill fast, and let the cups fly,
               And then let's get hence hastily.
               I must consider curiously
               Before these kings come back.

[Herod and his court withdraw. The Kings come forward. The star reappears and leads them on.]

FIRST KING: God, the most of might and main
               Who for mankind would suffer pain
               The star I see has come again
               Back into our sight.

SECOND KING: I hope without dread today
               To see that child in his array.
               But methinks lords, by my faith,
               The star is standing still.

THIRD KING: That is a sign that we be near.
               But no high hall doth greet us here.
               For a child of such power
               This housing is too low.

FIRST KING: I am certain this is he
               We seek here in this far country
               So now with all sincerity
               honour I pay that lord.

[They go into the stable to Joseph and Mary. The first King presents his gold]

               Hail be thou, Christ and Messiah.
               Well we know by prophecy
               That of the jews thou king shall be
               And mankind shall redeem.
               Therefore, as befits thy crown,
               Gold I give in my devotion,
               To honour thee in great renown,
               To recognise thy royalty.

SECOND KING: Hail to thee Christ Emmanuel.
               Thou art come, mankind to heal
               Of the sin where Adam fell.
               Incense now to thee I bring

In token of thy dignity,
Of thy office of spirituality.
Receive here Lord from me
My devoted offering.

THIRD KING: Hail conqueror of all mankind.
To show us mercy thou hast mind,
The devil's bond to unbind
By death to save our kind.
Myrrh to thee have I brought here
To balm thy body bright and fair.
Receive my present, sweetest sir,
And bless me with thy hand.

MARY: You royal kings in rich array,
To the high father of heaven I pray
To honour your good deed today
In his highest might.

May he ever give to you the grace
To earn the life that lasts always
And never to fall out of the faith
That in your hearts hold right.

JOSEPH: You kings full faithfully shall find
That God will have your deed in mind.
He was not gotten by love of kind -
And therefore be you bold.

But of the holy Ghost he is,
Come to bring mankind to bliss.
So this child is truly his.
So Gabriel me told.

ANGEL [GOBBET]:   I warn you comely kings all three
My lord would not let you slaughtered be.
And so he sends you word by me
To turn another way.
Herod's fellowship you shall flee.
Harm has he ordained for thee.
So go not through his country,
Not the way you came today.

FIRST KING: Ah high lord that we honour here,
Who warns us in this manner -
We will do all in our power
Thy bidding to fulfill.

SECOND KING: Farewell sir Jasper, brother, to you,
King of Tharsis most worthy.
Farewell sir Balthazar. To you I bow
I thank you of your company.

THIRD KING: May he that shaped both sea and sand
Send us safe into our land.

Kings two, give me both your hand.
Farewell and have good day.

[The Kings go. Herod and his court come forward.]

HEROD: Subjects all, hear my threat,
                Baron, burgess and baronet.
                That misbegotten marmoset
                Shall never master me.
                No puling page shall long enough be let
                To live to shove me from my state.
                To wage a war that shrew is set,
                To steal my sovereignty.

                Now those false kings have thought to flee.
                They were to show the child to me.
                It may now no other be
                But I must think again.
                All the boy children in this country
                Shall for his guile, I swear to thee,
                Because I know not which is he,
                All for his sake shall be slain.

                Now, pretty Pratt, my messenger.
                Come hither now, come to me here.
                Thou must now with ready cheer
                Get thee to Judee this day.
                Call all my brave and comely knights,
                Bid them haste with all their might
                Let them stay not, to brawl or fight.
                Bring them without delay.

MESSENGER: Yes my lord of great renown
                To do thy bidding I am bound,
                Lightly to leap over dale and down,
                And speed till I be there.

                How now, awake out of your sleep
                Sir Grimball and Sir Lancerdeep.
                Herod my lord sad care doth keep -
                Some knave would have his crown.

FIRST SOLDIER: Messenger, I will in all good faith
                Come with you upon your way.

SECOND SOLDIER: Right welcome are the words you say,
                that lord is of great renown.

MESSENGER: Hail great king who sits on high.
                Here are the knights of great degree,
                With full good will they come to thee
                To do whatever you say.

FIRST SOLDIER: Hail great king, crowned in gold.
                King and Caesar before thee quake.

SECOND SOLDIER: If any to fight you be so bold,
Sore strokes will he find for your sake.

HEROD: Welcome, so courteous both you be.
Yesterday to this city
There came to see us kings three
Who told us their intent -
To seek a child that born should be,
As was said in prophecy
To be king of Judee
And many another land.

Now alas, what may this be?
For I know not which is he.
So all the boy-children in this country
Must die under my hand.
Since we know not that child well,
Though we therefore go to hell,
All the children of Israel,
We doom them all to die.

FIRST SOLDIER: Alas my lord and king of bliss,
Send you after us for this?
A villainy full low it is
To slay a shit-arsed shrew.

SECOND SOLDIER: If he's a knight of champion
As strong and stiff as Samson,
For you I would beat him down.
But what you ask is shame to do.

HEROD: Nay, nay, it is not but one or two
That you shall slay, I swear to you,
But a thousand, even more -
Take that into your mind.
Because I know not which it is
Therefore, lest the child you miss
You must slay, I tell you this,
All that you can find.
You must walk far and near
Through Bethlehem.   For nothing spare
A boy child between two years
And one day old.

FIRST SOLDIER: It shall be done lord, by and by.
None will be left, certainly.
Soon shall we that shrew destroy,
And leave no child unslain.

The soldiers leave together

FIRST SOLDIER: If you would know my name aright
I am Sir Waradrake the knight.
No man dare against me fight.
My strokes strike them with dread.

Fierce am I to fight my fill,
As fierce as falcon is to fly.
I thirst to do my master's will
And drive those dogs to die.

Those creatures in their cribs I'll kill
And stoutly them destroy.
None shall escape, if I have my will.
I'll get that cursed boy.

SECOND SOLDIER: And see to me you take good keep.
My name is Sir Grimball Lancerdeep.
They that trouble me are laid to sleep,
They drop at every side.

Though the king of the Scots and all his host
Were here - I say without a boast -
I would ding down those laddies with might the most.
No man dare me abide.

FIRST SOLDIER: Farewell my lord and have good day.
I wish - I boast not by my faith -
That I might find Samson in my way,
To fight with him right here.

HEROD: Nay nay, I know, thou need not swear,
Thou art a doughty man of war.
But speed you fast, that is my prayer,
And come back fast again.

[The Soldiers set off towards Bethlehem. Herod withdraws.]

ANGEL [GOBBET]: Joseph, arise be not slow.
Into Egypt thou must go
And Mary too, to flee thy foe.
This is my lords will.
There stay, lest the child be slain,
Till I warn thee to come again.
False Herod uses might and main
Lord Jesus for to kill.

JOSEPH: Mary, sister, now we must flit.
Upon my ass shall thou sit.
Into Egypt we must get.
The angel will us lead.

MARY: Sir, for ever, loud or still,
I thy wishes will fulfill.
I know it is my lord's will.
I do as you have said.

They go. The angel sings and, if possible, on their way into Egypt a statue or idol falls down

FIRST SOLDIER: Have done fellows, hurry fast,
                   These carping queens must be down cast.

SECOND SOLDIER: Their children too must feel our thrust,
                   We've waited far too long.

FIRST WOMAN: Who call you queen, you scabby dog?
                   Thy dame, scum, may be such.
                   She might be some dirty bitch.
                   I tell thee I am none.

SECOND WOMAN: Be thou so bold, I'm warning thee
                   If you touch my son that is so sweet
                   This distaff and thy head shall meet,
                   Before you be done.

FIRST SOLDIER: Dame, be still and let me see,
                   If a boy that child there be.
                   The king has commanded me
                   All such to arrest.

FIRST WOMAN: Arrest? You are brave hunters, you two.
                   No wrong to us you'll do,
                   We can beat you black and blue,
                   Let us have our peace.

SECOND SOLDIER: Thy son, my lady, by my good faith,
                   I can teach a game to play.
                   He'll hop, before I go away
                   Upon my spear end.

FIRST WOMAN: Here's my answer, one two and three
                   Carry that to the king from me.

[She hits the soldiers.]

                   Tell him that's what I send.

FIRST SOLDIER: Come hither to me, my goodly wife

FIRST WOMAN: Leave my son, thou wicked thief,
                   If you do my child any grief
                   I shall crack thy crown.

The first soldier stabs the child with his spear

FIRST WOMAN: Out, alas, woe is me,
                   Thief, hanged thou shall be.
                   My child is dead. Now I see
                   My sorrow may not cease.
                   Have thou this, and thou this,
                   I'll beat the shit out of you, and the piss.
                   You may think we do amiss
                   But we'll not make our peace.

SECOND SOLDIER: Dame, show me thy child there
Now he must hop upon my spear.
If it any prick doth bear
I must teach him a game.

SECOND WOMAN: Nay fellow, there thou fails,
My child shall thou not assail.
It has two holes for its tail.
Kiss it, and you can see the same.

The second soldier stabs the second woman's baby

Out, out, out, out.
You shall be hanged for this you lout.
Thieves that you are, be never so stout
Full foul now have you done.

This child was given me
To look to, thieves, Who are ye?
He was not mine, as you shall see.
He was the king's son.

She goes to Herod

Look lord, look and see
The child that thou sent to me.
Men of thy own country
Have slain it - and here they be.

Herod is angry

HEROD: Fie whore, fie. God give thee pain.
Why said thou not the child was mine?
But it is vengeance, as I drink wine.
That I now can see.

SECOND WOMAN: Yes lord, they could have seen aright,
Thy son was like to be a knight,
In cloth of gold, and harness bright,
Painted wondrous gay.
Yet was I never so affright
As when they stabbed him in their spite.
Lord, so little was my might
When they began the affray.

HEROD: He was right fine in silk array,
In gold and pearl that was so gay.
They might well know as clear as day
He was a king's son.
What the devil is this to say?
Why were your wits so far away?
Could you not speak? Could you not pray,
And say it was my son?

What the devil can this mean?

My days now must be done.
I know I must die soon.
Fruitless is it to make moan.
Damned I must be.

My legs are rotting, and my arms.
Now I see the fiends in swarms.
I have done so many harm.
From hell they come for me.

I bequeath here in this place
My soul to Sir Sathanas.
I die now. Alas, alas,
Here I no longer dwell.

He shows signs of death. A Devil enters

DEVIL: Beware, beware, unwarily wakes your woe.
                    For I am swift as swiftest doe.
                    I come here for a king's soul,
                    I fetch a lord for hell.
                    All false believers I burn and blow
                    From the top of the head to the right toe.
                    All you who cheat will join him in woe.
                    There evermore to dwell.

                    And when I've lugged him down below
                    I'll come again and fetch some more,
                    As fast as I can go.
                    Farewell. Have a good day.

Exit devil

ANGEL [GOBBET]:   Joseph arise, and hurry.
                    Dead is your enemy.
                    Take Jesus and Mary
                    And go to Judee.

JOSEPH: Mary sister we must go
                    To the land that we came from
                    The angel has told us so,
                    My own dear sweet.

MARY: I thank you sir, all that I can.
                    He will guard us. He is God and man.
                    Hold the ass, while I get on,
                    That I may ride.

JOSEPH: Come thou here, my heart's dear root.
                    Full easily, sister will we go.
                    You can ride there every foot
                    And I'll walk by thy side.

ANGEL [GOBBET]:   Now you are ready for to go,
                    Joseph, Jesus and Mary also,
                    We will not leave you, but help you so

And keep you safe from all your foes.
We will make a melody
And sing with all this company
A word was said in prophecy.
A thousand years ago.

[The angel sings, and leads Mary and Joseph back to Judee.]

Original designs by Tony Lewery for the 1987 productions of the Chester plays

PART TWO
The Life of Christ

GOBBET:

You have seen already in this place
How Christ to save us through his grace
Came down to earth to keep God's promise,
As prophets before had said.
Now he begins his ministry of peace.
Actors here from Ashton Hayes
Will show how by Satan he tempted was,
And how a sinner was saved.

Original designs by Tony Lewery for the 1987 productions of the Chester plays

PLAY 8

The Temptation, and
The Woman Taken into Adultery

CAST: **Devil**
                        Jesus
                        Doctor [here Gobbet]
                        First Pharisee
                        Second Pharisee
                        Woman

The Devil enters

DEVIL: Now by my sovereignty I swear,
                        By the princely power that I bear
                        In hell-pain, when I am there,
                        A game will I begin.
                        See that man there, Sir Daisybeard,
                        That walks abroad both there and here.
                        He has no father that I can learn,
                        And his mother did no sin.

                        Ever since the world began
                        I never knew of such a man.
                        Greed or envy has he none,
                        Nor liking of lechery.
                        To hear him lie I never can,
                        I spy no sin that he hath done,
                        No treasure has he got from anyone,
                        No pride or gluttony.

                        By this my high state falls behind.
                        No fault in him can I find.
                        If he is God become mankind
                        My craft then fully fails.
                        More than man I know he is,
                        Or something he would do amiss.
                        Now I see he hungry is
                        But nothing else him ails.

                        And this thing truly dare I say,
                        If he be God, in good faith,
                        Hunger should hurt him in no way.
                        That were against all reason.
                        Let me see now if I may
                        With talk of bread this man betray.
                        For he has fasted many a day.
                        So bread is now in season.

The Devil speaks to Christ

                        Thou man, stay and speak with me.

If thou the son of God should be
Make from these stones - now let us see -
Bread, by thy blessing.

JESUS:

Satan, I tell thee truly,
Bread alone man lives not by.
But by God's words in certainty,
From God's mouth coming.

You waste your time then, Sathanas,
To try to push me from my place
By meat - as Adam was,
From paradise to pain.

Satan, for all your enticement
Hunger can not turn me from my intent.
For God's will omnipotent
Is a meat that will not fail.

DEVIL:

Out alas, What is this?
This matter goes all amiss.
Hungry I can see he is,
Just as a man should be.

By my cunning and my craftiness
I cannot turn his will in this.
No need of any bodily bliss
In him has he.

For he can suffer all annoy
As a man should, strong and sturdily,
But always he wins the victory,
As in him godhead were.

Trickery sly must I espy,
This disobedient to destroy.
He has mastery over me.
My fall begins, I fear.

Yet will I seek some subtelty.
Come forth, thou, Jesus, come with me
To this holy city.
I have an errand, I say.

If that truly God thou be,
Now I shall full well it see.
For I can grant great honour to thee
Before we go away.

Jesus stands on the topmost point of the temple

Say thou now, that sits so high:
If thou be God's son, by any way,
Come down. And I to thee will say
That thou has shown thy mastery.

Thine angels will keep thee.
Thou wilt not hurt thy foot nor knee.

Show thy power. Now let us see
What mastery may be granted thee.

Jesus speaks to the devil

JESUS: Satan, in certainty I thee say,
It is written that thou never may
Tempt God, thy lord, in any way,

What matter so ever be meant.

He comes down

DEVIL: Alas that woe is me today!
So I have failed to catch my prey.
I was never cast down at such a play,
Nor foiled of my intent.

Satan leads Jesus on to a mountain

DEVIL: But fellow, if it be thy will,
Go we and play upon a hill.
Another point I must fulfill
Whatever may befall.

Look about thee now and see
All this realm and royalty.
If you kneel down and honour me
You shall be lord of all.

JESUS: Go forth Satan, go forth, go.
It is written and shall be so,
'Thy God to honour shalt thou know,
To serve him, now and for aye'

DEVIL: Out alas, now must I quit.
Never I knew a man of such wit.
I must be punished in Hell-pit
For my reward and hire.

Alas that ever I was born
In sorrow I lie and shame and scorn.
With hell hounds will I be ragged and torn
And driven to the fire.

But I must hold to my intent.
To call a court full diligent,
Summon my servants to parliament
Before me to appear.

Then to reward with dignity
Those that all their life served me.
In burning bliss their shall they be,
And sit with Lucifer.

To you I leave my testament.
To all that in this presence sit,

To all these here, by my intent
Do I bequeath the shit.

The devil exits. The 'Doctor' comes on.

DOCTOR GOBBETT: So overcome thrice in this case
The devil was, as we showed in our play.
Of three sins Adam guilty was,
When the devil made him eat.

Adam was tempted in gluttony
When he ate of the fruit falsely,
And in avarice and vainglory,
Through eating of that meat.

Christ in those sins three
Was tempted, as you might well see.
Avarice pride and gluttony,
Brought Adam to his woe.

But Adam fell in his trespass
And Jesus withstood through grace -
For of his godhead in that place
The devil was made to know.

Two pharisees enter, leading a woman taken in adultery.

FIRST PHARISEE: Master, I say, by God almight,
That we lead the wretched wife
Who was taken tonight
In foul adultery
To Jesus, here in all men's sight.
That we can tempt him if we might,
To see if he will judge her right
Or else unlawfully.

SECOND PHARISEE: That is well said fellow, by my faith.
So might we catch him in some way.
For if he grants her grace today,
Our law is broken clean.

And if he bid us punish her sore,
He does against his own law,
As he has preached here before;
That mercy belongs to men.

They lead the woman to Jesus

FIRST PHARISEE: Master this woman that you see
Was wedded here, right lawfully,
But with another found her we,
And they did do amiss.

Moses law bids us stone
All such as be unclean.
So we bring her here to you alone
For judgement now on this.

Jesus writes in the earth

JESUS: Now which of you, everyone,
                     Is without sin, take him anon,
                     And cast the first stone.
                     Believe it, or be gone.

FIRST PHARISEE: Speak on master, something say.
                     Shall the woman be stoned, or nay?

                     Or have thou mercy, as thou may,
                     To forgive her this sin?

SECOND PHARISEE: Master, why art thou so still?
                     What writest thou, if it be thy will?
                     Shall we either keep or kill
                     This woman found in blame?

                     What write thou, master? Now let me see.
                     Out alas, that woe is me!
                     For no longer dare I here be,
                     For dread of worldly shame.

He flees

FIRST PHARISEE: Why now fellow, why does thou flee?
                     I will go to him and see.
                     Alas that I were gone away,
                     At least as far as France!

                     Stand you, sweeting, him beside,
                     No longer here dare I abide,
                     Against thee for to chide,
                     I go, while I have the chance.

He flees

JESUS: Woman, where be these men, each one
                     That put this guilt thee upon?
                     To damn thee now there is none
                     Of those there were before.

WOMAN: Lord, to damn me there is none.
                     For away they all be gone.

JESUS: Now I damn thee not woman.
                     Go forth and sin no more.

WOMAN: Ah, Lord, blessed must thou be,
                     That from mischief has helped me.
                     Henceforth filth I will flee
                     And serve thee in good faith.

                     For godhead full in thee I see
                     Thou know all things that do we.
                     I honour thee, kneeling on my knee,
                     And so will I do for aye.

DOCTOR [GOBBET]:   Now lords I pray you mark here,
The greatest goodness of God's deed.
I will make clear, if there is need,
The things that played were.

Jesus knew full well their thought
And all their wits he set at nought.
He bade who never had sin wrought
Cast first at her a stone.
He wrote in clay, believe you me,
Their own sins, that they might see
And each one was fast enough to flee,
And they left her alone.

Each one of them had the grace
To see their sins in that place.
Yet none of them the wiser was,
Though each of his own sin knew.

Full fast they were to take their way,
Lest they themselves were damned that day.
So helped he the woman, in good faith,
Our sweet Lord Jesu.

GOBBET: Jesus was a healer for everyone
When he his work on earth begun.
Now we shall go to Lazarus' tomb,
To see what he did there.
As Jesus saved all men from sin,
So gave he back our life again.
So players from Chester will show you, when
They play their pageant here.

PLAY 9

The Healing:
The Blind Man and Lazarus

CAST:

Jesus
Boy leading Blind man
Blind man
Two neighbours
Two Pharisees
Blind man's mother and father
Messenger
Mary
Martha
Peter
John
Thomas
Lazarus

JESUS:

Brethren, I am the son of God, the light of this world.
He that follows me walks not in darkness.
He has the light of life, as the scriptures record.
Patriarchs and prophets have told you of this.
Abraham, Isaac and Jacob to my coming bear witness.
To them I was promised before the world began,
To pay their ransom, to become a man.

All their testimonies tell you that I and my father are
    one.
He has sent me from the throne eternal
To preach and make clear his will unto man.
Because he loves him, above his creatures all,
As his treasure, his darling most principal.
Man, I say again, is his own, select,
Of all his creatures peculiarly elect.

And so it is my mind and will
That we go, my brethren, to Bethany,
My father's commandments all to fulfil.
I am the good shepherd, that puts his life in jeopardy
To save his flock, which I love so tenderly.
All the sheep will I guard, that are to me committed,
There is but one flock, and I am its shepherd.

Before we go, print these sayings on your mind and heart.
Record them and keep them in memory.
Continue in my word, do not from it depart.
Then shall all men know most perfectly
That you are my disciples and my family.
Do nought without me, let my word be your guide.
Then in your doings you shall always well speed.

[A blind man enters, led by a boy]

BOY: If pity may move your gentle hearts
                 Remember, good people, the poor and the blind.
                 With your charitable alms, give a poor man comfort.
                 He is your own neighbour, and of your own kind.

BLIND MAN: Your alms, good people, of charity,
                 To me that am blind, and did never see.
                 Your neighbour, born in this city.
                 Help me before I go.

PETER: Master, instruct us in this case
                 Why this man born blind was.
                 Is his parents sin or his the cause
                 That he has suffered so?

JESUS: It was neither for his offence
                 Nor for the sin of his parents
                 Or other fault or negligence
                 That he was blind born.
                 But for this cause specially;
                 To set forth God's great glory.
                 I prove to all God's potency,
                 When I his sight reform.

                 While the day is fair and bright
                 My father's works I must work right
                 Until the coming of the night
                 When light is gone away.
                 In this world, when I am here
                 I am the light that shines so clear.
                 My light to them shall well appear,
                 That light is mine, always.

Jesus spits on a piece of earth and makes mud. He rubs the blind man's eyes with it.

                 Do man as I say to thee.
                 Go to the water of Shiloh,
                 There wash thy eyes, and thou shalt see:
                 And give God all the praise.

The Blind man seeks the water. He goes away from Jesus. [Jesus withdraws.]

BLIND MAN: Lead me, good child, right hastily,
                 Unto the water of Shiloh.

He washes

BLIND MAN: Praised be God omnipotent
                 Which now to me my sight has sent.
                 I see all things here present.
                 Blessed be God always.

When I had done as God me bade
My perfect sight at once I had.
Therefore my heart is now so glad,
I know not where I am.

NEIGHBOUR 1:   Neighbour, and it's the truth I say -
This is the blind man who yesterday
Asked for alms as we came this way.
He is the very same.

NEIGHBOUR 2:   No no neighbour, it is not he.
But it is the most like him that ever I did see.
One man just like another may be,
And so were that man and him.

BLIND MAN: Good people truly I am he.
I was blind, and now I see.

NEIGHBOUR 1:   Explain that to us truthfully,
With no false reasoning.
How this happened, come on say,
And tell us the truth, we thee pray.
Thou who even yesterday
Could see no earthly thing.

BLIND MAN: The man which we call Jesus
That works miracles daily with us
And whom we find so gracious
Anointed my eyes with clay.
And to the waters of Shiloh
He bid me go immediately
And wash my eyes, and I should see.
And so I took my way.

When the water touched my eyes
Immediately I had my sight.
The joy I knew when I saw light
No man had known before.

NEIGHBOUR 2:   Where is he now, then, pray?

BLIND MAN: I know not where he is this day.

NEIGHBOUR 1:   Thou must come with us away,
And to the pharisees these words say.
But if thou would those things deny
It shall help thee right nought.

Look up lords, you judges of right.
We have brought you a man that had no sight.
One sabbath day, through one man's might
He was healed and restored, forsooth.

NEIGHBOUR 2:   Declare to them, you wicked man,
Who gave you back your sight again.

That we might find out, if we can,
Of this matter the truth.

BLIND MAN: Jesus anointed me with clay
And bade me wash in Shiloh,
And before I came away
My perfect sight I had.

PHARISEE 1:   This man, the truth if I should say,
Is not from God - my head I lay -
If he doth violate the sabbath day.
I judge him to be mad.

PHARISEE 2:   I cannot see it in my thought
That he which has this marvel wrought
Can be a sinner. I believe it nought,
It is not in my creed.
Say what it is that did thee heal.

BLIND MAN: A prophet he is without fail.

PHARISEE 1:   This fellow seems to my mind
A knave that's feigning to be blind.
The truth of this I aim to find,
To put us out of doubt.

Go forth messenger, far and wide,
And fetch his parents by and by.
This knave does nought but prate and lie.
I wish his eyes were out.

The messenger looks around for the blind man's parents

MESSENGER: Sir and dame, you that go there,
Before the pharisees you must appear.
What their will is, there shall you hear.
Have done, and come your way.

MOTHER: Alas man, what do we here,
Must we before the pharisees appear?
A vengeance on them far and near;
They never did poor men good.

FATHER: Dame, there is no other way.
Their commandment we must obey,
Or else they would, without delay,
Curse us and take our goods.

PHARISEE 1:   Come near to us, both of you.
Tell us truly, before we go,
Whether this is your son or no.
Be sure you tell no lies.

FATHER: To you my masters, we cannot deny
That he is our son, undoubtedly

But who restored him to his sight
Of him you must enquire.

MOTHER:
He is old enough his own tale to tell.
Maybe he could neither buy nor sell,
But he has his mother tongue to utter it well.
Let him speak, we desire.

PHARISEE 1:
Give praise to God, you crafty knave,
And see that hereafter you do not rave,
And say that Jesus did thee save.
Believe us, as is right.

PHARISEE 2:
He is a sinner. That we know.
Deceiving the people, to and fro.

BLIND MAN:
Whether he be a sinner I do not know.
He gave me back my sight.

PHARISEE 1:
What did he, you blabber-brain?

BLIND MAN:
I told you once, will you hear it again?
Or his disciples will you become,
Of all your sins to have remission?

PHARISEE 2:
O cursed caitiff, ill-hap to thee!
Would thou have us his disciples to be?
No, no! Moses' disciples we be,
For God to him did speak.

But such as this I never knew.

BLIND MAN:
I wonder at that, as I am true -
That you know not from whence he should be,
Who cured me, when I did never see.
To tell you this I dare be bold.
There is no man that ever could
Restore a creature to his sight
That was born blind, and never saw light.
Unless of God this Jesus is,
He could not work such things as this.

PHARISEE 1:
What, sinfull knave, will you teach us,
Who all the scriptures can discuss,
And of our living are so virtuous?
We curse thee out of this place.

[Jesus comes forward]

JESUS:
Believe thou in God's son truly?

BLIND MAN:
Yes gracious Lord. Who is he?

JESUS:
Thou hast seen him with thy eye.
He is the same that talks to thee.

BLIND MAN: Then here I honour him with heart free,
                    And ever shall serve him until I die.

JEW 1:   Say, man that makes such mastery,
                    Christ if that thou be.

JESUS: That I told you openly.
                    The works that I do before ye,
                    In my father's name almighty
                    Bear witness of me.

                    But you believe not what you see.
                    None of my sheep are ye.
                    I know my flock and they know me.
                    They answer to my voice.

                    No man shall take my sheep from me,
                    For my father in majesty
                    Is greater far than all ye,
                    Or any that ever was.

JEW 2:   Thou shall abide before thou pass.

                    Help fellow, and gather stones.
                    Beat him well and break his bones.

They collect stones

                    Why do we hear this ribald rave?
                    One stroke, as God me save,
                    This scorner sly will have.

JESUS: Wretches. Many a good deed
                    I have done, to those in need.
                    You give me foul reward
                    To stone me in this manner.

JEW 1:   Those good deeds that thou hast wrought
                    Are not the deeds we stone thee for.
                    Both in words and thought
                    Thou lieth there falsely.

JESUS: My father's bidding do I truly.
                    Since you will not believe me,
                    Not my deeds, that you may see,
                    Then learn of those that teach.

                    Then by their believing know you may,
                    That I am in my father alway
                    And he in I, as I thee say,
                    And each of us in each.

They pick up the stones and Jesus vanishes

JEW 2:   Out out alas, where is he gone?
                    He and all his men, each one

I would have taken them, right anon,
And battered them boldly here.

JEW 1:   Now by the death that I shall die,
I hope to see him with my eye.
To sir Caiaphas go shall I,
And tell him tidings dear.

[The Jews leave. Mary and Martha come forward, in 'Judee']

MARY: Ah Lord Jesus, that I feel such woe!
To see my brother sickly so!
A feeble time Christ chose to go.
We were well if he were here.

MARTHA: Yes, sister, I will go,
And look for Jesus to and fro.
If our case he were to know
Then would he help us here.

Jesus enters [in 'Bethany'. Mary goes over to him]

Ah my Lord. Sweet Jesus, mercy.
Lazar, that thou loved tenderly,
Lies sick, a little way near by.
And suffers in much pain.

JESUS: Woman I tell thee truthfully
That sickness is not deadly.
Gods son shall it glorify.
I am he, it shall be seen.

Martha goes up to Mary

MARY: Martha, sister, alas, alas.
My brother is dead since thou here was.
Had Jesus my Lord been here for this,
It had not so befallen.

MARTHA: Yes, sister, near is God's grace.
Many a man helped he has.
So may he help us in this case,
And to life our brother call.

MARY: Here will I sit and mourning make
Till Jesus might my burden break.
My pain to hear, Lord, thou take,
And ease me of my woe.

MARTHA: In sorrow and woe here will I wake,
And lament for Lazar my brother's sake.
Though I for cold and penance quake,
From here I will not go.

They sit together next to the tomb, weeping.

JESUS: Brethren, go we to Judee.

PETER: Master, right now thou well might see
                    The Jews would have stoned thee,
                    And yet thou will go again?

JESUS: Brethren, I tell thee tidings.
                    Lazar, my friend, is sleeping.
                    We must be going
                    Upon him I must call.

JOHN: Lord, if he sleep then safe is he,
                    For in his sleep no peril be.
                    Therefore it is not good for thee
                    To go for cause so small.

JESUS: I tell you brethren, certainly,
                    Lazarus is dead, and there go I.
                    That I was from there woe am I.

THOMAS: Follow him brethren. Bold must we be
                    To die with him devotedly.
                    Otherwise it will not be.

Jesus goes to where Martha and Mary are sitting:

MARTHA: Ah Lord Jesus, had thou here been laid,
                    Lazar my brother had not been dead.
                    But well I know thou will us aid,
                    Now thou art with us here.

                    This I believe and trust is right -
                    What thing thou ask of God almight
                    He will grant it from on high.
                    He will grant thee thy prayer.

JESUS: Thy brother, Martha, shall rise, I say.

MARTHA: I believe so Lord, in good faith.
                    He shall rise on the last day.
                    Then hope I him to see.

JESUS: Martha, to thee in truth I say,
                    I am the rising, the eternal day,
                    The life that shall last always,
                    And never shall ended be.

                    Whoever believeth steadfastly
                    In me - I tell thee truly -
                    Though he be dead and down he lie,
                    He shall live and fare well.

                    Believe thou, woman, that this may be?

MARTHA: Lord, I believe and put my trust upon,
                   The Christ, that thou art, God's son,
                   Who now into this world is come,
                   Man's blessing for to be.

                   This have I believed in steadfastly.
                   Therefore on me have mercy,
                   And on my sister Mary.
                   I will fetch her to thee.

Martha goes to Mary

MARTHA: Ah Mary, sister sweet and dear,
                   Hurry quickly, come here.
                   My sweet lord Jesus is near,
                   He calls upon thee.

MARY: Ah, well were we if so it were.
                   But had my lovely lord been here,
                   And seen my brother on his bier,
                   Then might some good be done.

Mary sees Jesus and lies down at his feet

                   Ah Lord Jesus, had thou been here
                   Lazarus my brother, thy own dear,
                   Had not been dead in this manner.
                   And we been saved our woe.

JESUS: Where have you put him? Tell me.

MARY: Lord, come hither and you will see.
                   Buried in this place is he,
                   Now four days ago.

The Jews enter

FIRST JEW: See, fellows, by cock's soul,
                   This lad begins to wail and yowl,
                   To sob and make great howl
                   For the man he loved before.

SECOND JEW: Had he the cunning, I think he might
                   From death have saved Lazarus by right,
                   As well as save that man his sight,
                   He that so blind was born.

JESUS: Have done, and put away the stone.

MARTHA: Ah Lord, four days are gone
                   Since he was buried, blood and bone.
                   He stinks Lord, in good faith.

JESUS: Martha, said I not to thee
                   If thou fully believed in me

God's grace soon should thou see?
Therefore do as I thee say.

They lift the stone from the tomb. Jesus turns his back and raises his arms.

JESUS: Father of heaven My thanks to thee
                    That so soon has heard me.
                    Well I know and truly see
                    Thou hearest my intent.
                    But for these people that stand nearby
                    Speak I to thee openly
                    That they may believe steadfastly
                    That from thee I was sent.

                    Lazarus, come forth, I bid thee.

LAZARUS: Ah Lord, blessed must thou be
                    From death to life thou raisest me
                    In thy marvellous might.
                    Lord, when I heard the voice of thee,
                    All Hell failed of majesty
                    So fast from them my soul would fly
                    All devils were afraid.

JESUS: Loose him now and let him go.

MARTHA: Ah Lord, all honour be to thou
                    That save us from our woe
                    Well I knew it should be so,
                    For so has it been before.

MARY: Lord Jesus I thank thee
                    That on my brother thou had pity.
                    In clear signs now men may see
                    That thou art God's son.

                    With thee lord ever will I be
                    And serve thee with a heart so free.
                    This day hast thou gladdened me.
                    Always with thee I go.

JESUS: Good days be yours, my daughter dear
                    Wherever you go, far or near.
                    My blessing I give you here.
                    To Jerusalem take we our way.

GOBBET:

The mighty city of Jerusalem
Will now before your eyes be seen.
To it Lord Jesus in triumph comes,
Lord of heaven and earth.
But fear and envy mark his way.
All men are not his friends today,
As young actors from this town will say,
As they act both woe and mirth.

PLAY 10

Judas

CAST: Simon the leper
              Lazarus
              Martha
              Mary of Magdalen
              Judas
              Jesus
              Peter
              Philip
              A Janitor
              Four citizens
              Two children
              Two traders
              Caiaphas
              Annas
              Two pharisees

Jesus and his disciples enter the house of Simon the leper.

SIMON: Welcome Jesus, full of grace.
              Poxed and measled once I was.
              But thou Lord, healed me has,
              All over, as I can show.

              Good it is to see thy face
              Here in my house, this poor place.
              Thou art my comfort in many a case,
              That I full well know.

LAZARUS: Welcome to me, sweet Lord Jesu.
              Blessed is the time that I thee knew.
              From death I rose through thy virtue,
              To live and see thy face.

MARTHA: Welcome and sit, if your will it were,
              And I shall help to serve you here.
              as I used to do so, in the same manner
              Before, in another place.

Jesus sits down, and all sit with him. The Magdalen comes in with an alabaster jar of ointment.

MAGDALEN: Welcome to you my lovely lord.
              Welcome my heart, welcome my health.
              Welcome all my worlds wealth,
              My blessing and my bliss.

From thee lord can I not conceal
My filth and all my faults frail.
Forgive me that my flesh doth fail,
That to thee I do amiss.

Ointment I have here ready
To anoint thy sweet body.
I am wretched and unworthy,
But tell me not to go.

Full of sin and sorrow am I.
But for that I am sorry.
Amend me in thy mercy.
Be gentle to my woe.

She opens the box and makes signs of using the ointment. She washes the feet of Jesus with her tears, and dries them with her hair.

SIMON: Ah Judas, why doth Jesus so?
I think that he should let her go,
This woman full of sin and woe,
For fear of worldly shame.

If Jesus a true prophet were
He should know of her life here,
And suffer her not to come him near,
For that might spoil his fame.

JUDAS: Nay brother Simon, sooth to say,
Please me it nothing may
To see this woman pour away
An oil of so much price.

This box of ointment might be sold
For three hundred pennies, all told,
And given to poor men if we would.
We should be more wise.

JESUS: Simon, take good heed to me.
I have a tale to tell to thee.

SIMON: Master, what your tale may be
Say on, I beseech.

JESUS: Two debtors once there were
Owed money to a usurer.
One of these two debtors
Owed five hundred pence all told.
The other, fifty, as I say here.
They were poor, so at their prayer
He forgave them both, right there,
And took nothing of their gold.

Which of these two - say if you can -
Was more beholden to that man?

SIMON:

Five hundred is more than fifty.
So I think certainly
The greater the sum that in debt was he
The more beholden he was.

JESUS:

Simon, thou judgeth right in this.
Seest thou how this woman is?
She has not done amiss
To treat me in this manner.
When I came here, and you did greet,
No water was there for my feet.
She washed them with her tears wet,
And wiped them with her hair.

Kiss when I came thou gave me none,
But since this woman here has come,
She has kissed my feet each one.
Her weeping never ceased.
With oil thou did not me anoint,
But she hath soothed both limb and joint.
And Judas, why stick you at that point,
When this woman has me eased?

A good deed she hath done today.
The poor you have with you always,
Me ye may not have, by my faith,
But for a little space.

Therefore woman, know by me –
Thou hast loved so tenderly
All thy sins now forgive I.
Belief hath saved thee.

And all that tell of me truthfully
Throughout the world by and by
Shall hold thy deed in memory
And tell what thou did for me.

MAGDALEN:

My Christ, my comfort and my king,
I worship thee in all things.
For now is my heart rejoicing
And bliss is mine above.

Seven devils now, as I well see,
Hast thou driven out of me.
From foul life into purity
Thou relieved me lord, for love.

Jesus gets up.

JESUS:

Peter and Philip, my brethren free,
Before you a castle you may see.
Go you there and fetch for me
An ass and a foal also.
Loose them, bring them here anon.
If any man grudge you either one,
You say that I will ride thereon.

Soon they will let them go.

PETER: Master, we shall do your bidding,
                    And bring them here for anything.
                    Philip, brother, let us be going,
                    And fetch these beasts two.

They go into the city. Peter says to the janitor:

How, how! I must have this ass.

JANITOR: You get off me neither that nor less.
                    Tell me, before I let you pass
                    Where they are to go.

PHILIP: My master Jesus, believe you me,
                    Thinks to come to this city
                    And said both brought to him should be,
                    Himself to ride upon.

JANITOR: They are ready, good men, in good faith.
                    And since he will come today,
                    To all in this city I will say
                    To wait on his coming.
                    Take ass and foal and go your way.
                    Each man on Jesus marvel may,
                    Lazarus lay dead for full four days,
                    But he raised at his calling.

The janitor goes to the citizens.

Tidings, good men every one.
The prophet Jesus comes anon.
Truly he is God's son,
As all of us must say.

FIRST CITIZEN: Ah lord, blessed must thou be.
                    Him will I go now and see.

SECOND CITIZEN: Fellows, I believe that Christ is he,
                    That did such marvels day by day.

THIRD CITIZEN: Branches from the palm tree
                    Each one in his hand take he
                    And welcome him to this city
                    In fair procession.

FOURTH CITIZEN: With all the honour that I may
                    Will I welcome him today
                    And spread my clothes before his way
                    To greet him in this town.

FIRST CHILD: Fellows, I heard my father say
                    Jesus the prophet will come today.

SECOND CHILD: Sing hosanna along the way
                  With branches in our hands.

The children go towards Jerusalem singing Hosanna and holding palm branches in their hands. The citizens spread clothing in his way, and shout 'Hosanna to the son of David, blessed is he who comes in the name of the lord, Hosanna in the highest! '

JESUS: Ah, Jerusalem, holy city.
                  Unknown today it is to thee
                  That thou art at peace - thou canst not see.
                  But woe waits far and wide.
                  Much must thou dread some other day,
                  When doom shall fall on every way,
                  And thou bewildered, sooth to say,
                  With sorrow on all sides
                  Destroyed, to darkness driven down.
                  No stone with other in this town
                  Shall stand. None here are bound
                  By Christ's commandment,
                  By God's own visitation,
                  Done for mankind's salvation.
                  None here know true devotion,
                  Nor dread they his high doom.

Jesus rides towards the city, and all the citizens spread their cloaks in front of him. He goes to the temple, gets down from the ass and speaks to the traders, with a whip.

                  Go away, use not these things.
                  It is not to my liking.
                  You make my fathers dwelling
                  A place of merchandize.

FIRST TRADER: What fool is this that spoils our fair
                  And casts down all our stalls and ware
                  No man has ever come here
                  To insult us in this way.

SECOND TRADER: Out, out, woe is me.
                  My table and my money
                  Are spread around for all to see.
                  But I dare nothing say.

FIRST TRADER: Say Jesus, for all thy jangling,
                  What evidence or tokening
                  Says that you can act the king.
                  How dare you. Come now, say.

JESUS: This temple here I could destroy
                  Through my might and majesty.
                  I tell you now, in days three
                  I shall build it up again.

FIRST TRADER: Aha Jesus, will thou so?
                   These words, as quick as I can go
                   Shall be said again before some more.
                   Caiaphas I shall tell.

Jesus drives the traders out with the whip.

JESUS: Fast from this temple see you go
                   Buying and selling shall be here no more.
                   In this place, complain you ever so
                   You can no longer dwell.

JUDAS: By dear God in majesty
                   I am as angry as I may be.
                   Some way I will avenge me
                   As soon as ever I may.
                   My master Jesus, as men might see,
                   Was rubbed, head foot and knee,
                   With oil worth all our treasury
                   I should not have seen that day.

                   Whatever was given to Jesu
                   I have looked after, since I him knew,
                   He takes me to be true.
                   His purse I always bear.
                   He had been better, in good faith
                   To keep the ointment that day.
                   Somehow I will make him pay
                   For the waste that was done there.

                   Three hundred pennies worth it was
                   That he let spill in that place.
                   Therefore let God give me hard grace
                   If he now be not sold
                   To Caiaphas, when his council sits,
                   For the tenth part of it.
                   And so my master shall have quit
                   My grief a hundred fold.

Judas exits [to re-enter later in the scene, or withdraws]. Caiaphas enters [to Annas and the Pharisees].

CAIAPHAS: Lords, upholders of the law,
                   Listen, all gathered here before.
                   All men Jesus to him draws,
                   All in his power he has.
                   If we let him long go on
                   All men will believe in him anon.
                   Then shall the Romans come along
                   And push us from our place.

                   Therefore now it must be said -
                   Let us see how to have him dead.
                   If he must longer his life here leads,
                   Our law goes all to nought.

And so let each one give his counsel
What is the way will best avail
To force this wicked shrew to fail.
Some trick there must be sought.

ANNAS

Sir you speak right skilfully
But we waste our time on him to spy.
We catch him in no villainy.
Our traps and tricks all fail.
For you know as well as I,
Often to harm him have we tried,
But he always has the victory.
That no man may avail.

FIRST PHARISEE:

Yes lords, one point must be made again.
That layabout Lazarus should be slain.
Jesus raised him up again,
That four days had been dead.
For once that miracle was known,
Honours were paid him by everyone.
Lazarus was dead, but he won't lie down,
While Jesus lives, as I've said.

CAIAPHAS:

No more, forsooth, will many more,
That he has made to speak and go,
The blind that have their sight also,
Love him steadfastly.
They follow him both far and near,
Preaching to the people of his power.
And so my wit is in despair,
To find a remedy.

ANNAS:

But some remedy must there be,
Before this great solemnity,
Or many others as well as we
Must pack up and take their way.
For when he comes to this city
All the world as you might see,
Honoured him upon their knees
As if God were come that day.

SECOND PHARISEE:If he heals or raises any more
All men will believe his law.
So it is good that he be killed before.
There is no more to say.

CAIAPHAS:

Put your wits together and let us see
If we can take him with some subtelty.
We can give silver and gold for fee,
To whomever can do our will.

JUDAS:

What my lords will you give me?
I shall soon help, and he
Right slyly betrayed shall be,

Your wishes to fulfill.

CAIAPHAS: Welcome fellow, and well met too.
              That bargain will I make with you.

JUDAS: Let me see what you will do.
              Lay down silver here.
              The devil can fry me in his fire
              If I do it without hire
              Either for sovereign or for sire.
              It is not my manner.

CAIAPHAS: Say on what we shall give thee
              To make certain that he taken be.
              And here is ready money,
              To pay thee before.

JUDAS: As ever I may thrive, or thee,
              Before I show my subtelty
              Thirty pence you must give me,
              And not a farthing less.

FIRST PHARISEE: Yes, but your truth to us must be plight
                 Your promise to give us our right,
                 To betray your master through your might
                 And then you'll have money.

JUDAS: Have my true oath. I'll see you right.
              On Friday, before it's night
              I shall bring you to his sight
              And tell you which is he.

FIRST PHARISEE: You are all alike as brothers in a row.
                 Which he is I cannot know.

JUDAS: No. A true sign I shall show.
              See whom I kiss.
              That is he, sooth to say.
              Take him as manfully as you may,
              Lead him quietly away,
              Where your purpose is.

CAIAPHAS: Now look thou serve us truly
              Of thy masters coming be our spy.

JUDAS: Believe me now. In certainty
              Jesus will I bring to you.

              On Friday in the morning
              I think to eat with him and drink.
              And after tiding to you bring.
              Trust me. I will be true.

                         INTERVAL

PLAY 11

The Last Supper

CAST:

Jesus
Peter
John
Servant [here, Gobbet]
Master of the house
Andrew
Judas
Thomas
Philip
Malchus
Jew

JESUS:

Brethren all, to me right dear,
Come to me and you shall hear.
The feast of Easter draws near,
You know it is at hand.
Celebrate that feast will we
With very great solemnity
The pascal lamb must eaten be
As the law commands.

Therefore Peter, off you go
And John with thee also.
Make all things fit, as you know how,
According to the law.

PETER:

But tell us Lord where the feast will be.

JESUS:

Into that city go speedily.
A man with a water pot you shall see.
By that sign you may him know.
Into a house you will see him go.
Into that house you will enter also.
Say the master sent you two,
That this is his bidding that you do.

Say 'To thee our master has us sent
To find a place convenient
The paschal lamb to eat'. That is my intent,
To eat there with you all.

Peter and John go and find the man with the water pot [here Gobbet].

PETER:

All hail good fellow, heartily.
Go to thy masters house, go hastily.
We will keep you company.

SERVANT ⌊GOBBET⌋ Come on your way and follow me.
Say now what you will.

They go into the house.

PETER: Sir, the master salutes thee.
                  His two messengers are we.
                  A place prepared for him must there be,
                  To eat the paschal lamb.

MASTER OF THE
HOUSEHOLD: Look, here is a parlour all neat and bright,
                  With paved floors, and windows light.
                  Make all things ready as you think right,
                  All things shall be done.

JOHN: Now brother Peter, all is ready.

They prepare the table and go back to the others.

PETER: Thy commandment, Lord, done have we.
                  Therefore come on, and you shall see.
                  We will lead the way.

JESUS: Now brothers, go you to your seats.
                  This paschal lamb now let us eat.
                  Then we shall eat of other meat
                  And feed on truth this day.
                  Now must you know, the time is come
                  That signs and shadows all are gone.
                  We must make haste, that we may soon
                  Cast riddles and hints away.

                  A new law now must I begin,
                  To help mankind out of his sin,
                  So that he may heaven win,
                  Which he for sin has lost.
                  And here in presence of you all
                  Another sacrifice begin I shall,
                  To save mankind from Adam's fall,
                  To help him as I must.

Jesus sits down, and John falls asleep in his lap.

                  Brothers, I tell you by and by
                  With great desire desired have I
                  To eat with you here holily
                  Before my passion.
                  I say to you in certainty
                  My father's will almighty
                  I must fulfill all meekly
                  And ever to him be bound.

Jesus takes the bread, breaks it, and gives it to the disciples.

This bread give I here my blessing.
Take and eat it, brothers, at my bidding.
Believe you, without doubting,
This is my body
That shall die for all mankind
In remission of man's sin.
This I give you, to keep in mind,
Now and for evermore.

He takes the cup in his hand and raises his eyes to heaven.

Father of heaven I thank thee
For all that ever thou dost to me.
Brothers, take this with hearts free.
That is my blood.
It shall be shed upon the tree.
Drink together no more shall we
Till in heaven's bliss we be,
And taste that ghostly food.

He eats and drinks with his disciples. Judas has his hand in the bowl.

Brothers, in truth to you I say
One of you shall me betray.
One that eats with me today.
One of this company.

PETER: Alas, alas, what can I say?
I know not the man who may.
It is not I, in all good faith.
Who could do this to thee?

ANDREW: It is hard for us all
That such an evil shall befall.
We are but twelve within this hall.
Lord tell me if it be I.

JESUS: Through his deceit I am already dead,
He that in my cup now wets his bread.

JUDAS: Dear master, is it not I
That shall do you this villainy?

JESUS: You know it Judas, for certainty.
You are he.
What you will do, do speedily.

JUDAS: Farewell to all this company.
For on an errand I must fly.
Left undone it may not be.

JESUS: Leave your meat, brothers. I will begin
To wash your feet, everyone,
Always keep my deed in mind,
And humbler will you be.

Jesus wraps a towel around his waist

PETER: Nay lord, by no means and in no manner
                Will you wash my feet here.

JESUS: Unless I wash you, have a care,
                Of joy you get no part.

PETER: But not my feet, Lord as I have said,
                Wash my hands and wash my head.

JESUS: All must be clean. Do not dread.
                Give your feet to me.

Jesus washes the feet of all the disciples one by one.

JESUS: My little children, my brothers free,
                A little while with you may I be.
                You cannot go from here with me,
                Nor follow me on my way.
                But do this at my bidding.
                Love each the other in all things,
                As I myself, without flinching
                Love you truly always.

                So shall all men know and see,
                That you my true disciples be
                When falsehood you are seen to flee,
                When you love well together.

PETER: Lord, where leads that path you take today?

JESUS: Peter, where I go this day
                You cannot follow. Sometime you may,
                But not now, in no manner.
                One day thither thou shalt go.

PETER: Why not Lord, why is it so?
                For thee would I lead a life of woe,
                For thy sake would I be slain.

JESUS: Peter, I say in certainty,
                Before the cock has crowed cries three,
                Thou shalt forsake my company
                And take back thy words again.

                Brothers, let not your hearts be sore.
                Believe in God for evermore.
                Believe in me, as you have before,
                And care not in this case.
                For in my father's house there is
                Many a mansion of great bliss.
                There I go, remember this,
                To pick you out a place.

And though from you I go away
I come again some other day.

THOMAS: Tell us, let us know the way,
That all of us may go with thee.

JESUS: To know my father truly
You must know him first in me.
I am the truth, the life, the way.

PHILIP: Lord let us see thy father anon.
That were enough for everyone.

JESUS: A long time with me have you gone.
Then, Philip, why say you so?
I tell you truth, who looks on me
Looks on my father. I ask of thee,
Why must you my father see
When I am here with you?

All the works I do are his.
Help from him I could not miss.
To win yourselves heaven's bliss,
You must have faith in me.

Whatever you ask my father dear
In my name, in good manner,
To do thy wish I have the power.
All that you saw me do and say
Was done that my father in majesty
Glorified the more might be.
And I too, as I say to thee.
For we are one, always.

Rise up. Let us go from here anon.
To my prayers I must be gone.
You stay still there, everyone,
While I on my father call.
Stay awake. Have my blessing and benison
To keep you from temptation.
The spirit quick to sin is found
The flesh is fast to fall.

Jesus goes [to 'Gethsemane'] to pray. The disciples, in their sorrow, fall asleep.

Father of heaven in majesty,
Glorify, if thy will it be,
Thy son, that he may glorify thee.
Now or soon thy power send.
Thou gave me might on earth, and majesty.
I have done with a heart free
The work with which you charged me,
And brought it to an end.

Thy name I have made men to know
And slackened not thy will to show

To my disciples wherever I go.
That power hast thou given me.
And now they know for certainty
That by the father sent am I.
Therefore I pray to thee heartily
Save them, in thy mercy.

He goes to his disciples and finds them sleeping.

What, sleep you all, my brothers here?
Rise up now and say your prayers,
Lest temptation have the power
To make you fall.
The flesh is, as I said before
Always inclined to sin right sore.
The spirit must struggle, evermore,
So wake up, one and all.

He returns to his prayers and says in a loud voice.

My heart is full of foreboding.
My death is coming.
Father, dare I ask this thing,
That thou put it away from me?
Nothing to thee impossible is.
Nevertheless, now in this
At your will my spirit is.
As you will, so let it be.

He goes back to the disciples.

You are sleeping, brothers still I see.
Sleep on now, all of ye.
My time is come to taken be,
From you I must away.
He that hath betrayed me,
This night from him I will not flee.
In a sad time born was he.
So he will live to say.

Judas enters with a band of soldiers, carrying lanterns, sticks and weapons.

JESUS: You men, I ask you, whom seek ye?

MALCHUS: Jesus of Nazareth, him seek we.

JESUS: Here. All ready. I am he.
                    What have you to say?

JUDAS: Ah sweet master, kiss me.
                    It has been long since I saw thee.
                    Come away from here with me,
                    Come. Let us steal away.

JESUS: What seek you men, so out of breath?

FIRST JEW: We seek Jesus of Nazareth.

JESUS: I said before and still I say
                  I am he, in all good faith.
                  Let these men go on their way.
                  And I am at your will.

MALCHUS: False thief. Thou shall be gone
                  To bishop Caiaphas, and that anon.
                  I'll break thy body, every bone,
                  If you're a moment late.

PETER: Thief yourself, be not so bold,
                  My master with thy hands to hold.
                  I'll punish you a hundred fold.
                  To start with, take thou that.

He draws his sword and cuts off Malchus' ear.

                  Go and complain to Caiaphas.
                  Tell him to make it right.

MALCHUS: Out alas, alas alas,
                  By Cock's bones, my ear he has.
                  I wish I had never, in this case,
                  Come with the others here.

JESUS: Peter, hold not thy sword so high.
                  Whoever takes the sword and fights with it gladly
                  Shall die by the sword, and die right quickly.
                  Put it up, you need not fear.

Jesus takes up the ear and heals it.

MALCHUS: Ah well am I now, well am I,
                  My ear is mended now I see.
                  Right merciful a man is he.
                  I never knew such a one.

FIRST JEW: He may have healed thee,
                  But safe from us he cannot be.
                  To Sir Caiaphas, I say to thee,
                  He with us must go.

JESUS: To catch a thief you came here,
                  With swords and staffs and armoury.
                  To take me foully, in base manner
                  To wreak thy wicked will.
                  I was in the temple that other day.
                  No hand on me then would you lay.
                  The time is come now, now the day,
                  Your intentions to fulfill.

FIRST JEW: Come caitiff, come to Caiaphas
Or thou shall feel our grievous grace.
Trot along now, make a prouder pace,
Thou poor man's pope.

Sir Beelzebub, Sir Sathanas
Might come to help thee in this case.
But both those hands your holiness has
Must fast be bound with rope.

PLAY 12

The Trial

CAST: Four Jews
         Annas
         Caiaphas
         Jesus
         Pilate
         Herod
         A Damsel
         Peter
         (Fifth Jew)
         [Two women of Jerusalem
         Simon of Surrey (Cyrene) [here, Gobbet]; see note at end of
         play]

The Jews lead Jesus before Annas and Caiaphas.

FIRST JEW: Lord Bishop, here have we brought
              A wicked wretch, much mischief has he wrought.
              He would bring our laws to naught.
              With scorn our power he spurns.

SECOND JEW: Yes, far and wide we have him sought,
              His presence here was dearly bought.
              A great many men in deed and thought
              To his will has he turned.

ANNAS: Oh, jangling Jesus, are you now here?
              Now you can prove your privy power.
              Can you make your cause all clean and clear?
              Thy Christhood we must know.

CAIAPHAS: He'd be a master conjurer
              If for a penny, a pound or a prayer
              He could get himself shut of his danger
              And some trickery show.

ANNAS: Sir it is needful - this will I say -
              That we here in this company
              This Sir Daisybeard destroy,
              If we want our people saved.

THIRD JEW: Sir Caiaphas, listen now to me.
              This babbling buffoon our king would be.
              I don't care what he says to thee.
              I have heard him say before
              That such was his power and majesty
              The Temple to destroy could he,

And build it up in days three
Right as it was of yore.

FOURTH JEW: Yes, that was what I heard him say.
He cannot deny it by no way.
Also, that he was God, I say,
Emmanuel and Messiah.
He can't dodge that one, he can't deny.
Forty more, as well as I
That were in the temple on that day
They heard him, in good faith.

CAIAPHAS: So Jesus, what say ye?
You know what is said against thee.
Put forth thy might, thy majesty,
Prove to us thy power.
What, devil? Not one word speaks he.
Jesus, here I conjure thee -
That you are God's son, here before me,
I challenge you to swear.

JESUS: As you say, just so say I.
I am the son of God almighty.
I tell you truly,
Once again you shall me see,
On God's right hand, in majesty,
Man to judge in clouds of glory.

CAIAPHAS: Judge us? Fie on thee, fie on thee, fie.
Bear witness, all this company.
Full falsely lies he.
What he has said all of you hear.
What need of witnesses is there?
We are gathered altogether
And hear how loud he lies.
What say you, what say that are here?

FIRST JEW: Beat him and buffet him, fill him with fear.
A new law he can learn,
If he wants our law destroyed.

CAIAPHAS: He shall not destroy it.
Spite him, mock him, scorn him, spit.

ANNAS: Let us see him hit.
Punch him in the face.

The Jews sit Jesus in a chair.

FIRST JEW: For all the harm he's done here,
He must be the devils dear.
Let's look at him. Come on, come more near.
See the fool that calls us false.

SECOND JEW: He's famous now, I fear.
Let's see who's bold enough to hit him here,
Spit at him, all together.
Come on, buffet him, all.

THIRD JEW
(spitting):   You heard him all in this place just now.
You him, how he lied just now,
Right in the middle of his face, right now,
I'll foully defile him.

FOURTH JEW
(spitting):   He shall have a slap now
God he makes himself now
He can get no grace now.
Watch me beguile him.

FIRST JEW
(hitting him):   Fie on thee, freak,
Stoop now and squeak,
Your brains will break
Now, I'll be bound.

The second Jew [blindfolds Jesus and] hits him on the face.

SECOND JEW: A veil will I take
To cover his face,
Let's see if he will make
A little more sound.

THIRD JEW: If thou be messiah,
Unless you are a liar,
Tell us who hit thee - I desire
To know. Are you the Christ?

FOURTH JEW: For all his prophecy,
There he fails thee.
Watch my fists fly,
I'll give him a feast.

FIRST JEW
(hitting him):   My punch will bite,
I'll beat him to shit
No man has my wit
In doing him woe.

SECOND JEW: I can't see him flit.
He's had it too light.
Let's show him our spite.
He ought to have more.

THIRD JEW: Much more may he have from me.
Soon I will see
If I can make thee pay,
Great prince, on thy pate.

FOURTH JEW: If he say nay
                I shall, in faith
                Lay on. I say -
                It's still not too late.

They stop hitting him.

CAIAPHAS: Sir, what do you now advise?
                This man should be dead, if we were wise.

ANNAS: Lead him before the high justice.
                Lord Pilate knows the law.

They lead Jesus to Pilate.

CAIAPHAS.   Sir Pilate, here we bring a man
                Known to be false, our elders' foe.
                For tribute, he would give Caesar none,
                This man that stands here.

ANNAS: Wherever he and his fellows go
                They turn folks' minds. They say that he is king also.
                Such a man we must not let go,
                When we have him in our power.

PILATE: What say you, man of misery?
                Are you the king of the jews? Say.

JESUS: So you say. All men may
                Hear you make me a king.

PILATE: I can see no cause, I say in good faith,
                To do this man to death today.

CAIAPHAS: Sir. All the people go his way.
                They follow him in everything.

ANNAS: Yes. All the land of Galilee
                Turned clean towards his law has he.
                So now we ask of thee -
                Do this false man down.

PILATE: Since he was born there - so you say
                Then send to Herod he should be.
                Otherwise I offend Herod's royalty
                I blemish his renown.

                Go, take him to Herod, hurry.
                Say that he is sent from me.
                Herod, in his majesty,
                Can act at his own liking.

FIRST JEW: Herod shall have him hastily.
                I'll take him there, so say I.
                Come on - and none of your ribaldry.

When you speak to our king.

The Jews lead Jesus to Herod.

FIRST JEW: Lord, King, Pilate to you has sent
                     A villain who holds our law in contempt.
                     He wants you to give judgement
                     Before we take him away.

HEROD: Ah, welcome Jesus. I consent.
                     Thank Pilate for his present.
                     For a long time now I've meant
                     To have you brought my way.

                     Jesus, much have I heard of thee.
                     Some magic power I'd love to see.
                     If you from God in majesty
                     Have come, tell us here.

                     I beg you, say it now to me.
                     Give us a taste of your wizardry.
                     A lot happier I would be,
                     In all honesty, it would make my year.

Jesus says nothing.

HEROD:
                     What. I think the man is mad.
                     Or dumb, and that's no good.
                     No scallywag like him before me stood,
                     Not as stout and stern as he.
                     Carry on, Jesus. God's blood,
                     Pilate I tell you never would
                     Hurt you. But you must mend your mood.
                     And say something to me.

                     Alas I am nearly mad myself for woe.
                     He's dumb, he's deaf, he's frantic too.
                     But Pilate forgives him. I will also.
                     I let him go, after today.

                     Clothe him in white. In his case
                     It may please Pilate. The custom it was
                     To dress madmen in white. Look at his face.
                     It suits him, in good faith.

The Jews dress Jesus in a white robe.

FIRST JEW: Have this, Jesus. Put it on thee.
                     It's a king's livery.

SECOND JEW: Now we can see your royalty.
                     Thank Herod for this gift.

They take Jesus to Pilate.

FIRST JEW: Lord Pilate, the king has sent
Jesus back again. When we went
To him, he forgave his bad intent.
As you did that same day.

PILATE: Yes. Faults in him I can find none.
Nor can Herod, nor can anyone.
So its best we let him be gone,
Wherever he takes his way.

SECOND JEW: Nay, all of us, all cry in one voice,
Nail him, nail him to the cross.

PILATE: Gentlemen, for shame. Stop that noise.
My counsel is this, I say.
All of you know the usual manner.
We set free a prisoner
On the feast that now approaches near,
In honour of that day.

Is it your will that Jesus be set free?

THIRD JEW: No. Worthy to suffer death is he.
And so all of us cry to thee -
Barabas should be saved.

PILATE: What will I do with Jesus then?
Christ is he called and King of men.

FOURTH JEW: Nail him on a cross. For all his sin
That is what he deserves.

PILATE: Now I see you all so fervent,
And on this man's destruction bent,
I will wash my hands here in your presence,
Though you make yourselves run mad.
I offer you this testament
That I am clean and innocent,
That I will not shed by my own intent
A righteous man's blood.

Pilate washes his hands. Caiaphas and Annas withdraw with Pilate.

PILATE: You prelates tell me now, each one -
What will you do? Will you let him be gone?

CAIAPHAS: Nay. Nail him to the cross anon,
Doom him, before you're gone.

PILATE: You take him, if you are so grim.
According to your law, you judge him.

ANNAS: No, that is not lawful. Neither life nor limb
Can we take from a man.

PILATE: What the devil of hell is this you say?
                   Jesus, tell me now, I pray,
                   Are you the king - say yes or nay -
                   Of the Jews, by ancestry?

JESUS: Do you think that so it be?
                   Or did somebody tell it thee?

PILATE: No in faith. You yourself can know and see
                   No Jew am I.

                   Men of thine own nation
                   Have demanded thy damnation.
                   With many an accusation
                   Have they called on me all day.
                   Are you their king? Tell me. Whatever they cry.

JESUS: My realm is not of this world. So say I.
                   It is not, but it might be, certainly,
                   If these men would know my way.
                   And if my realm of this world were,
                   I would fight with you here,
                   I would lead such a power
                   To destroy your kingly sway.
                   But my might in this manner
                   I may not manifest, nor appear
                   As an earthly king. My cause unclear
                   Would be then, in good faith.

PILATE: Ergo, a king thou art. Or was.

JESUS: You say it. I say no less.
                   My presence to thee must express
                   That I am king, and king may be.
                   I came to the world to bear witness
                   Of truth, so, born I was.
                   All that believe in truthfulness
                   Take heed of what I say.

PILATE: What is truth? Tell me.

JESUS: Truth comes from God's authority.

PILATE: On earth, does truth lack majesty,
                   In your opinion.

JESUS: How could it be
                   That truth knew power and majesty
                   On earth, when here on earth is he
                   Who is truth, but is judged, against reason.

PILATE: Lords, I find no cause, in this,
                   To damn this man. Here he is.

CAIAPHAS: Pilate, he has done amiss.
                    He has broken Moses' law.

ANNAS: Pilate, he who makes himself appear
                    A king, takes some of Caesar's power.

PILATE: Go then. Scourge the troublemaker.
                    Beat him, whip him sore.

FIRST JEW: Come on, take care,
                    Cast off thy wear.

SECOND JEW: On thy body bare
                    Our strokes will tear.

They strip him and tie him to a pillar.

THIRD JEW: Now is he bounden
                    Now woefully wounded.

FOURTH JEW: No lad from here to London,
                    Could lash like me - within the law.

After they have whipped him they dress him in purple and sit him on a throne.

FIRST JEW: Now since he king is,
                    Beggar, I, bring thee this.

The second Jew puts a crown of thorns on his head.

SECOND JEW: Of thorns this thing is
                    For thee to wear.

THIRD JEW: Have here a reed,
                    Your sceptre to be.

FOURTH JEW: Beg pardon for our deeds.
                    All fall on our knees.

FIRST JEW: Hail King of the Jews.
                    See the reverence we show.

SECOND JEW: Rebel, see in sorrow,
                    The price of thy offence.

THIRD JEW: Let's write it on his face.
                    This is your oil of grace .

[They spit in his face]

FOURTH JEW: All the balm you get is this,
                    This is our reverence.

PILATE:	Lords. Here you can see Your king, in all his royalty.
CAIAPHAS:	Nay sir, forsooth, no king have we Save the emperor of Rome, his majesty. Unless you nail him on a tree, The emperor full of wrath will be.
ANNAS:	All of us say the same as he. Judge him while you've still got time.
PILATE:	Which of them would you rather have, Christ or Barabas.
CAIAPHAS:	Jesus is a traitor. All such as he Must be nailed up on a tree. Let Barabas go on his way.
PILATE:	Take him, now I say. He cannot be saved, That would be the end of me.
FIRST JEW:	The trial is at an end.

The second Jew brings a cross on, on his back.

SECOND JEW:	Come here, behind. Stop your back. Bend. Here may thou not abide.

They start out for Calvary.

DAMSEL (To Peter):	Weren't you with Jesus of Nazareth?
PETER:	I know him not, nor what thou said.
DAMSEL:	Look, I tell you plain This man here is one of them. He was with him in the garden. I know that's true.
PETER:	It is not true, I swear to thee. I know him not, in the slightest degree.
JEW:	You are one of them surely, You are from Galilee, Your speech gives you away, In front of us all.
PETER:	In faith and truth, that is not so. Let it be my shame, let it be my woe, If ever before I did him know, Or keep him company.

Note: The following is part of the Crucifixion play (Play 13) to be played at the 1987 Chester production as the end of Part Two.

CAIAPHAS:

Jesus - would you be our king?
Go forth! An evil way will we thee bring
You will be ruined, right to our liking,
Revenged full soon will we be.

Spur him on fast, make him go,
This fellow was our wise men's foe.
Your wicked wiles won't win you from woe,
No man can help you from harm.

ANNAS:

He seems to be weary of his way.
Come here, you, Simon of Surrey,
Go with him to Calvary,
Help him his cross to bear.

SIMON [GOBBET]:

The devil take this company.
For death he is not worthy.
For his sake, truly,
I think you all are lost.

CAIAPHAS:

Simon, unless its your intent,
To bear this cross on your back bent,
You'll suffer pain and imprisonment,
For all your bluster and boast.

SIMON [GOBBET]:

Alas, that I ever left my home.
Would to God I had been in Rome,
And never to this place had come,
Like this to be annoyed.
I call to God to witness,
I do this under your duress.
All of you, for your falseness,
I hope you're all destroyed.

ANNAS:

Have done. Bring forth those thieves two.
On either side of them they shall go.
This fellow will have friends to go
In fellowship together.

FIRST WOMAN:

Alas, alas, and woe is me.
A heavy sight is this to see.
So many of the sick saved he,
And now he goes this way.

SECOND WOMAN:

Sorrowful may his mother be,
To see his flesh, so fair and free,
Nailed so foully on a tree,
As he must be today.

JESUS:

You women of Jerusalem,
Weep not for me. The time will come
When tears for your own children

You will shed tenderly.
The time will come to you, I swear,
To bless the belly that never bore,
To thank the breasts that no milk came near,
So great your misery.

PART THREE
The Redemption of Mankind

Original designs by Tony Lewery for the 1987 productions of the Chester plays

PLAY 13
The Crufixion

CAST:

Caiaphas
Annas
[Simon of Surrey (Cyrene) [here, Gobbet]; see note]
Two women
Four Jews
Pilate
Mary, the Mother of Christ
Mary Magdalen [The sister of Martha]
Mary Jacobi
Mary Salome
Two Thieves
John
Centurion
Longinus [a blind soldier]
Joseph of Arimathea
Nicodemus [here Gobbet]

Note: The section in square brackets in the Chester 1987 production is played at the end of Part Two, but omitted in Part Three.

[CAIAPHAS:
Jesus - would you be our king?
Go forth! An evil way will we thee bring
You will be ruined, right to our liking,
Revenged full soon will we be.

Spur him on fast, make him go,
This fellow was our wise men's foe.
Your wicked wiles won't win you from woe,
No man can help you from harm.

ANNAS:
He seems to be weary of his way.
Come here, you, Simon of Surrey,
Go with him to Calvary,
Help him his cross to bear.

SIMON:
The devil take this company.
For death he is not worthy.
For his sake, truly,
I think you all are lost.

CAIAPHAS:
Simon, unless its your intent,
To bear this cross on your back bent,
You'll suffer pain and imprisonment,
For all your bluster and boast.

SIMON [GOBBET]:   Alas, that I ever left my home.
                   Would to God I had been in Rome,
                   And never to this place had come,
                   Like this to be annoyed.
                   I call to God to witness,
                   I do this under your duress.
                   All of you, for your falseness,
                   I hope you're all destroyed.

ANNAS: Have done.£ Bring forth those thieves two.
                   On either side of him they shall go.
                   This fellow will have friends to go
                   In fellowship together.

FIRST WOMAN: Alas, alas, and woe is me.
                   A heavy sight is this to see.
                   So many of the sick saved he,
                   And now he goes this way.

SECOND WOMAN: Sorrowful may his mother be,
                   To see his flesh, so fair and free,
                   Nailed so foully on a tree,
                   As he must be today.

JESUS: You women of Jerusalem,
                   Weep not for me. The time will come
                   When tears for your own children
                   You will shed tenderly.
                   The time will come to you, I swear,
                   To bless the belly that never bore,
                   To thank the breasts that no milk came near,
                   So great your misery.

CAIAPHAS: Come on, tormentors, do me right,
                   Strip and spoil him that did us spite.

FIRST JEW: I'll beat his lordship into shite
                   I'll see him shaken.
                   Does the king need the help of a serving man?
                   I will be his chamberlain.
                   Come sir. You'll never see this coat again,
                   Till you awaken.

[He takes off Jesus' coat]

SECOND JEW: That coat should be mine.
                   It's good and fine.
                   There's no seam therein,
                   That I can see.

THIRD JEW: God give thee pain,
                   If that be thine.

You're always inclined
To take things on thee.

FOURTH JEW: Nay fellows, by this day,
At the dice we will play,
And let them say
Who has the coat.

FIRST JEW: Right, by my faith,
That was well said.
Lay out the clothes,
Lay them all out.

They strip Jesus of his clothes. He stands naked while they throw the dice.

SECOND JEW: Now fellows, let us see.
Here are the dice, one, two three.
Which of all we
Will win this wear?

THIRD JEW: Nay, divided they should be,
Parted equally,
So I say to thee,
Before we go further -

FOURTH JEW: This coat has no seam,
To rip it were a shame,
For in all Jerusalem
There is no such garment.

FIRST JEW: His other clothes all
To us four shall fall.
First part them I shall
And after play for this
This shirt belongs to me.
You have the jacket for your fee.

To the third -

This belt is for thee.

To the fourth -

And you can have this.

SECOND JEW: Now let us sit down and see
Whose the coat we saved will be.

They sit down. The First Jew throws the dice [and loses].

SECOND JEW: My father's kin, it's not for thee,
This coat shall be mine.

Right! I humbly pray,
Grant me all doubles here today.

He throws [and loses].

THIRD JEW: You fail, fellow, by my faith.
                  Have this for your fee.

                  So go on your way,
                  As well you may,
                  Go off, I say,
                  Leave this with me.

[He throws and loses then the Fourth throws and wins]

FOURTH JEW: Look fellows, why don't we just agree
                  To hand the garment over to me.
                  God himself says as much to thee -
                  Look - there's his judgement.

FIRST JEW: Well let's have the grace to say
                  You've won the toss today.
                  All sixes there, what can we say.
                  Go on, take the garment.

CAIAPHAS: Come on men, for God's sake.
                  How long will peewee arse
                  Stand naked in this place.
                  Go and nail him on the tree.

SECOND JEW: Anon, master, anon anon.
                  If we need a hammer, here is one
                  Far and wide you may be gone,
                  But you'll never find such another.

THIRD JEW: Here we are now, by my bones,
                  Nails, very good ones,
                  To fix him on,
                  Though he were my brother.

FOURTH JEW: Let's get going fast.
                  Here's rope that will last.

FIRST JEW: That will draw him to the mast.
                  Let's get on with our play.

SECOND JEW: Lay him on,
                  This foolish man.
                  I will drive one
                  Of the nails in at the end.

They put him on the cross.

THIRD JEW: Yes, but see,
                  Short armed is he.
                  He won't fit on the tree.
                  Something will have to mend.

FOURTH JEW: Ah, worry ye not.
                  A trick I've got.

                        Some ropes must be brought
                        To stretch him by strength.

FIRST JEW: Pull, for your father's kin,
                        While I drive in
                        An iron pin,
                        To stake him out at length.

They fix his right hand down, and pull at the left with the cords.

SECOND JEW: Now fellows, by this light
                        His feet should be fastened right.
                        To do this properly, as we might,
                        Up he must be raised.

THIRD JEW: Pull him up on high,
                        Before your very eyes
                        Nail his feet down firm will I.
                        I think I've earned some praise.

They nail down his feet.

FOURTH JEW: Fellows, can you see
                        How I stretched his knee.
                        So why don't you praise me?
                        I've done well too.

Pilate comes over with a placard in his hand.

PILATE: Come here you, I command thee.
                        Nail this notice on the tree.
                        King of the Jews he would be,
                        So he must have his heraldry.
                        ' Jesus of Nazareth' - here, you can see,
                        ' King of the Jews'. How like it thee?
                        It's written there, for so said he -
                        Every word, exactly.

SECOND JEW: Nay sir Pilate, so God me speed,
                        You have done a sorry deed.
                        King is he none, but all now can read
                        That he was king of the Jews.

PILATE: That which is written, so have I written.

THIRD JEW: Yes, and I wish you were beshitten,
                        For that is foully written.
                        What the devil a king was he, man?

They lift up the cross, and Mary comes in weeping.

MARY the mother of
Christ: Alas my love, my life forlorn,
                        Alas my woe, my time to mourn,

To find my son tugged, lugged here, roughly torn,
By traitors to be slain,
With nails thrust in and crown of thorn.
So must I sorrow, evening and morn,
To see the fruit that I had borne,
To suffer new pain.

My sorrow, sweet son, I pray thee cease,
Or from my life grant me release.
How should I pass my time in peace
To see thee in such penance?
To be thy mother thou me chose,
And of my body born thou was.
As I conceived thee sinless,
Show me thy allegiance.

Alas the sorrow of this sight
Marrs my mind in main and might.
But still my heart methinks is light
To look on that I love.
Thieves, alas why do ye so?
Kill me, and let my son go.
For him would I suffer all this woe,
And meet again above.

MARY MAGDALEN: Alas, how can my heart be light
To see my Lord in such a sight,
For him I fail, but God rules right,
He'll give you much mischance.

MARY JACOBI: Help me Lord, do something.
Out of this bitterness to bliss me bring,
Or slay me now, for anything,
To save me from this strife.

MARY SALOME: Come down, Lord, and break thy bonds,
Loose and heal thy lovely hands.
Tell me Lord, why bear thou wounds,
Since thou art God and life?

ANNAS: Now this shrew has been hoisted on high,
I would see, for all his trickery sly,
How for his crown he means to fight,
And far from us all to flee.
He that has healed so many a one,
Now let him save himself, if he can,
Then we will all believe in him,
And know God's son is he.

JESUS: Father of heaven, if thy will it be,
Forgive them what they do to me.
They are blind. They cannot see
How foully they do amiss.

CAIAPHAS: If you have the potency,
And are God's son in majesty,
Come down, and we will believe in thee,
And say that it is so.

FIRST THIEF: If thou be Christ, to thee I say,
Now, God's son, find some way
To save us from our deaths today,
And thyself also.

SECOND THIEF: Ah man, be still, I thee pray.
Fear God, I tell you, always.
You speak in folly, by my faith.
Make not your friend your foe.

Man, you know well how it is,
It is right we suffer this,
But he has not done such amiss,
To suffer so painfully.
Lord I beseech thee,
When you come into your majesty,
Think on me.
On me have mercy.

JESUS: Man, I tell you in good faith,
Because of your belief I say
In paradise thou shalt be today,
With me in bliss.
And woman, to thee I say,
A son there next to thee may thou see,
That virgin clean has been always,
Right as thyself is.

And John, there thy mother may thou see.

JOHN: Yes Lord, her keeper I shall be.
Welcome Mary, mother free.
Together we must go.

MARY the Mother of
Christ: Alas my heart will break in three.
Alas, death, I call on thee.
My son, take thou this life from me,
Sever me from this woe.

JOHN: Comfort thee now, sweet Mary.
Alive shalt thou him see,
Rising with full victory.
When he fulfills the prophecy.
Thy son shalt thou see, certainly,
Within these days three.

JESUS: Eloi, Eloi, My God, I speak to thee.
Eloi lama sabachthani.
Why hast thou forsaken me?

FIRST JEW: Hark, hark how he cries on Eli,
              To deliver him hastily.

SECOND JEW: Yes, and we'll soon see,
              Whether Eli dare come or no.

JESUS: My thirst is sore, my thirst is sore.

THIRD JEW: And you will have some drink therefore.

[he offers Jesus a sponge on a stick, with vinegar and gall]

              You won't have the taste to drink any more,
              For seven long years or so.

JESUS: Mighty God in majesty,
              To work thy will would I never end.
              My spirit I give up to thee.
              Take it Lord, in thy hands.

              Consummatum est.

CENTURION: Lords, I tell you truly,
              This was God's son almighty.
              I know by the manner of his cry -
              He has fulfilled the prophecy,
              For needs so it must be.

CAIAPHAS: Centurion, as God me speed,
              You must be fuddled. You are deceived.
              But when you see his heart bleed,
              Let's see what you can say.
              Longinus, take this spear in hand
              And push it away from thee - make a wound.

LONGINUS: Ah Lord, I have seen neither sea nor land
              This seven year in good faith.

FOURTH JEW: Hold the spear and take good heed.
              You must do what the bishop bade.
              Of this thing there is great need.
              I think you must be mad.

LONGINUS: I will do as you tell me,
              But at your peril shall it be.
              What I do I cannot see,
              Whether it be evil or good.

Longinus pierces Christ's side with the spear.

LONGINUS: High king of heaven, thy word I hear.
              On my hand and on my spear
              Water from thy side is running clear.
              What I have done I do not know.
              On my eyes it falls.

I can see both one and all.
Ah Lord, wherever is the well
Where these waters flow.

Alas, alas, what have I done today.
A man I see, that I have slain.
For mercy Lord, to thee I pray,
I know not what I did.
Thee will I serve and with thee be,
That healed the sick and the blind in thy pity,
That will rise in days three,
As I believe, for so thou said.

JOSEPH: Ah Lord God, what hearts have ye
                 To slay this man that I here see,
                 Dead, hanging on the rood-tree,
                 Who never did amiss.
                 Certainly God's son is he.
                 There is a tomb made for me,
                 Where his body lain may be,
                 For he is king of bliss.

NICODEMUS [GOBBET]: Sir Joseph, I shall help thee.
                 Go ask Pilate for his body
                 And buried he shall be,
                 Though Caiaphas go horn-mad thereby.

Joseph goes to Pilate

JOSEPH: Sir Pilate, as a special favour I thee pray,
                 To grant me a boon, as I know thou may.
                 This prophet that is dead today - may I have his body?

PILATE: Joseph, why not, in good faith.
                 If the Centurion is prepared to say
                 That he is dead, without delay
                 Thy wish I grant fully.

                 Centurion, is Jesus dead?

CENTURION: As sure sir as I eat my bread.
                 No life in him is left.
                 I stood right by.

PILATE: Joseph, take him then with thee,
                 Bury him wherever it pleases thee.

JOSEPH: Thank you sir, certainly.
                 My good wishes go with thee.

Joseph goes up to Calvary [and, with Nicodemus and the disciples, takes Jesus from the cross]

JOSEPH: Ah Sweet Jesu, Sweet Jesu,
                 As thou art God, faithful and true,

In a tomb, made full new,
Thy body will be laid.
So Jesus, come, come here to me.
Thy blessed body buried shall be
With all the worship and decency
That men to thee can pay.

NICODEMUS [GOBBET]:   Joseph brother, well I see,
This holy prophet is given to thee.
For wondrous signs might all men see
When he gave up the ghost.
The sun lost all its light,
Graves opened in men's sight,
The dead did rise, earth quaked in fright,
He is of might the most.

NICODEMUS [here,   Therefore here brought have I
JOSEPH]   A hundred pounds of spicery,
Myrrh, aloes, and many more thereby,
To honour him will I bring,
To balm his sweet body,
When in sepulchre he lies,
That he may have mercy
When he is heaven's king.

———————

GOBBET: Our actors have told of evil and good -
How Jesus on the cross withstood
The shedding of his precious blood,
To save all of us now here.
After his passion
He broke Hell for our redemption.
Of that the teachers from here around
Will teach you with full good cheer.

PLAY 14

The Harrowing of Hell

CAST:
Adam
Esau
Simeon
John the Baptist
David
Satan
Two Devils
Jesus
The Archangel Michael
The Thief
An ale wife

ADAM:
O lord and sovereign saviour,
Our comfort and our counsellor,
Thou alone art authour
Of this thy heavenly light.

A sign it is of succour
To thy folk that live in langour.
Thou art the devil's conqueror
As we shall see in sight.

Me thou made, Lord, out of clay,
And gave me paradise in to play.
But through my sin, in sorrow I say
Deprived I was by thee

From that bliss was I cast away.
Here have I lingered since that day
In this distress, both night and day,
With all my family.

Now, by the light that now I see,
Joy is come Lord, all through thee.
On thy people thou hast pity,
To put them from their pain.

Surely it cannot other be
But thou hast mercy now on me.
Through thy will all my family
Thou may restore again.

ESAU:
Yes certainly, this very light
Comes from God's son, lord of might.
For so I, Esau, prophesied aright
While I was living.

Then men who live in darkness, by my prophecy,

Shall see great light. This is no lie.
So in my book have written I,
For every man's reading.

SIMEON:

And I , Simeon, sooth to say,
Will honour God all that I may.
For when he child was, in good faith,
In temple I him took.

There I prayed for my release,
That God would let me be in peace,
For he is Christ that came in grace,
As men may find in book.

JOHN THE BAPTIST:

Lord, I am that prophet John
That baptised thee in the flood of Jordan
And prophesied to every nation
To warn of thy coming.

To bring the people to salvation
By merit of thy bitter passion,
Through faith and penance to have remission
And with thee to have living.

When I lived in wilderness
These words did I then rehearse -
The lamb shall bring forgiveness,
Our ransom for to be.

All kneel

DAVID:

High God and King of Bliss,
Worshipped be thy name for this.
I hope that time now coming is
To fetch us from our fear.

Come Lord, come to hell anon,
And take thy folk out everyone.
Year after year has come and gone,
Since mankind first was here.

Satan addresses the demons from his throne

SATAN:

Hell hounds all that haunt here
Make you bold with snarl and sneer
For to our fellowship of fear
There comes a visitor.

A noble morsel you can have.
Jesus, the son of God above
Comes down with us to live.
Let him feel our wrath full sore.

Man is he fully, by my faith,
Greatly dreaded he death today,
And these words I heard him say
'My soul is sore to death'.

Such as I made halt and blind,
He has healed in proper kind.
Therefore this boaster look ye bind
In bale of hell breath.

FIRST DEMON: Sir Sathanas, what man is he
That should demean thy majesty,
How dares he do against thee,
Yet dread his death today?

Greater than thou he seems to be.
Degraded of thy high degree
Must thou be soon, full well I see,
Deprived of all thy prey.

SECOND DEMON: Who is he so stiff and strong
That comes so masterlike us among?
He shall sing a sorry song.
But what if it befall -

SATAN: Against this shrew that cometh here
I tempted the folk in foul manner.
They gave him for his dinner
Vinegar and gall.

Then they hanged him on a tree.
Now he is dead, all through me,
And anon, as you shall see,
Hell-ward cometh he.

FIRST DEMON: Sir Sathanas, is not this the sire
That raised old Lazarus from the fire?

SATAN: Yes. This is he that would conspire
Anon to rule us all.

SECOND DEMON: Out out! Alas alas!
Here I conjure thee, Sathanas,
Thou suffer him not to come in this place,
For aught that may befall.

Jesus enters. There is a loud cry, or noise.

JESUS: Open up the gates of hell,
You princes of pain that in darkness dwell.
The son of God enters, know this well.
He is the King of bliss.

FIRST DEMON: Go hence, upstart, out of this place
Or thou shalt have a sorry grace.
For all thy boast and menaces
These men must thou miss.

SATAN: Out alas, what is this?
Saw I never so much bliss

Coming unto hell like this
Since I've been warden here.

My mastery all goes amiss.
For yonder a stubborn fellow is.
He acts as though all Hell were his,
To push me from my power.

SECOND DEMON: Satan, now fails thy sovereignty.
Go forth, fight for thy degree,
Or else our prince thou shalt not be,
From here then thou must flit.

Satan rushes from his seat

SATAN: Alas I fail, Alas, alas.
My mighty power fallen has.
This prince that now in presence is
Will pull me from my prey.

Adam by my cunning tempted was.
His blood through me all fell from Grace.
Now plucked they all are from this place
Where I must ever dwell.

DAVID: I King David now well may say
My prophecy is fulfilled, this day.
I taught all men to hold in faith
That God should conquer hell.

Jesus speaks again

JESUS: Open up Hell gates, again I say
You princes of pain that are present.
And let the King of bliss this way,
To work his full intent.

SATAN: Stay, what is that king of bliss?

DAVID: The lord of might he is.
There is no power like to his.
To bliss he will man bring.

Jesus takes out Adam. The other Patriarchs follow

JESUS: Peace to thee, Adam my darling.
And peace to all thy off-spring,
That righteous were in living.
From me you shall not sever.

To bliss I will you bring.
There you shall be without ending.
Michael, lead these men singing
To bliss that lasts forever.

MICHAEL: Lord, your will fulfilled shall be.

Come forth Adam, come with me.
My Lord upon the rood tree
You safe from sin hath bought.

Now shall all happiness come to thee,
You are restored to your degree,
Though Satan with his subtlety
From pride to pain you brought.

SATAN: Out alas. Now go away
All my prisoners and my prey.
I myself may not start away.
I am so stoutly tied.

Now that Christ comes, sorrow may I
For myself and my men for aye.
Never since God made the first day
Were we so sore afraid.

ADAM: Sir, what manner of man be ye?

THIEF: My father Adam I say to thee
I am that thief that hung on the tree.
When in my heart I knew God's son
To him devoutly did I pray.
And he answered, and said, 'This day
With me in paradise shalt thou play'
And hither have I come.

He taught me by this tokening,
This cross upon my back hanging,
That Michael the angel would me bring
To give me entry.

ADAM: Now go we to bliss, old and young,
And worship God all willingly.
And our way now let us sing
With great solemnity.

**They all go. Michael begins the 'Te Deum Laudamus'. [The Ale-wife enters, still
in Hell]**

WOMAN: Woe be the time that I came here -
So I say to thee now Lucifer
And to thy fellowship all together,
All present in this place.

One time I was a taverner,
A good gossip, and a tapster,
For wine and ale a trusty brewer
And that my woe hath wrought.

For of cans I kept false measure.
Cupfulls I sold at my pleasure,
Deceiving many a creature,
And all my ale was naught.

And when I'd been a brewer long,
I used the hops to make ale strong,
Ashes and herbs I'd mix 'em among,
And so marred much good malt.

And so may I my hands well wring,
Shake out my cups and cans ring.
Sorrowfull may I sigh and sing,
That ever I that way dealt.

Taverners and tapsters of this city -
You'll all be promoted here with me,
If you break the rules of the country,
And cheat us with bad ale.

All tapsters who think you're cunning,
Marring the malt and brewing thin,
Selling small measure, money to win,
All who falsely deal,

All you who water your wine in the night,
Brewing and blending before it be light,
Faking a claret that causes full right
Much sickness and disease.

All of you take yourselves, more and less
To my sweet master, Sir Sathanas,
To dwell with him in his place -
Whenever it may you please.

SATAN: Welcome dear daughter, to us, all three.
                    Though Jesus took most of our company,
                    You can abide here still with me,
                    In pain without an end.

FIRST DEMON: Welcome, sweet Lady. I will thee wed.
                    Many a heavy and drunken head
                    Because of thy ale was brought to bed,
                    Far worse than any beast.

SECOND DEMON: Welcome, dear darling, to endless hell.
                    Cards and Dice you tricked with, and cups too small.
                    With many false oaths you sold your ale.
                    Now you shall have a feast!

GOBBET: The scholars of Chester college are bound
           Great of worship and renown,
           To show us the Resurrection.
           Fair may it them befall.

PLAY 15

Resurrection

CAST: Pilate
Caiaphas
Annas

                         (Colphram
Three soldiers   (Jeregras
                         (Aroysias
Jesus
Two angels
Mary Jacobi
Mary Salome
Mary Magdalen   [The sister of Martha]
Peter
John

PILATE: Lord Caesar, mightiest in majesty,
Honoured my state and my degree.
When they sent that Jesus to me
To deliver him up to death,
They cried on me all with one voice.
The Jews against me made great noise.
I let them hang him on a cross.

I fear that he might still us grieve.
What I saw I well believe.
I saw the stones in shards to cleave,
And dead men up to rise.
In this city all about
No one was so stern or stout
To dare to watch or walk about
So sharp was their surprise.

And so sir Caiaphas, I dread
That there was danger in that deed.
I saw him hang on cross and bleed
Till all his blood was shed.
And when he did his death take
The light waned, the sky waxed black.
Lightning, thunder, the earth began to quake -
And so I am afraid.

CAIAPHAS: And this was yesterday, about noon?

PILATE: Yes, sir bishop, that's the one
We must consider what's to be done.
I let them bury him full soon
In a tomb of stone.

And therefore sirs, between us three,
Let us ordain and oversee
If any danger be.
And then let us begone.

CAIAPHAS: Sir Pilate, all this was done
As we saw it ended soon.
Later in the afternoon
The weather began to clear.
And sir, if it be your will
Such words you speak - let them lie still.
Hide your thoughts and use your skill,
Lest any man should hear.

ANNAS: Yes, sir Pilate, careful be.
I saw him and his company
Raise men by sorcery
That long before were dead.
If there be any more such left
Who know of such witchcraft,
And his body went from us by theft -
Be careful, as I've said.

CAIAPHAS: Yes, sir Pilate, I tell you right.
Call you together many a hard knight,
Well armed to stand and fight
With power and with force.
Then no shame will us befall.
Let us decide between us all.
On true men let us call
To keep well the corpse.

PILATE: By Jesus - now that he is dead -
I think your counsel wondrous good.
The best men in kin and blood
To us three will I call.
Sir Colphram and sir Jeregras
And you, the bold Aroysias -,
We pray you sirs, here in this case
Do not hold back at all.
My knights, all stiff and stern of heart,
You are bold men and you are smart.
I warn you now, sharp and short,
What you have to do.

FIRST SOLDIER: We all be here, everyone,
Bold men to your service bound,
To drive your foes and bang them down
As long as we may stand.

PILATE: That I well do understand .
Men you are of doughty hand.
My love will you never lack.

That prophet that to death was drawn
Under sentence of our laws
Somehow puts me still in awe
For words that he did speak.
This in truth I heard him say,
That he would rise the third day.
Surely now, and so he may.
He knows some wondrous tricks.

SECOND SOLDIER: Yes, let him rise up, Hardly,
With my fellows here, and I.
He can't awake and slip us by.
He won't get off uncaught.

THIRD SOLDIER: I helped to slay him, not long ago.
Thinks he still to plague us so?
I bet my head the answer's no.
Ban danger from thy thought.

FIRST SOLDIER: Have good day sir.
We will be gone.
Give us your orders to each one.

PILATE: Now farewell, the best in blood and bone,
And take good heed to what I say.
I swear now that I tell you true
If that you any treason do
Not one, no single one of you
Will live to walk away.

[Pilate withdraws. The Soldiers go over to the tomb.]

SECOND SOLDIER: Well now fellows, the stakes are high
Our prince has sworn that we shall die
Without excuse or reason why
If we fail in our duty.
We must take care, if we be wise.
Let us think hard, as I advise.
Though he be bold, he cannot rise
But one of us must see.

THIRD SOLDIER: Sir, the most wit lies in thee.
You give the orders and oversee.
You are the eldest of us three,
A man of most renown.
The tomb is here at our hand.
Tell us now where we must stand.
If he rise we shall be found
Ready to beat him down.

FIRST SOLDIER: And I shall now set us so
That if he rise and tries to go
One of us, or else two
Shall see his rising up.

Stand thou there and thou here
And I myself in the middle there
I know our hearts need have no fear
They're made of sterner stuff.

The angels sing and Christ rises. He puts his foot on the soldiers.

JESUS: Earthly man that I have wrought
Awake out of thy sleep.
Earthly man that I have bought
No thought of me thou keeps.
From heaven I came, man's soul I sought
Down in a dungeon deep.
My dearest love from thence I brought.
For woe of her I weep.

I am perfect prince of peace
And king of free mercy.
Who from sin will have release
On me they call and cry.
And if they will from sinning cease
Peace I grant them truly.
And to that end the richest feast
Of bread, of my own body.
I am blessed bread of life
From heaven I was sent.
Who eats that bread, man or wife,
Shall live with me, without an end.
That bread that unto you I give
Your wicked life to amend
Becomes my flesh through your belief
And doth release your sinful bond.

Who eats that bread in wicked life
He receiveth his own death -
I warn both man and wife.
The which bread will be seen instead
From joy to turn to grief.
When he is dead, who foully fed
He goes to pain and strife.

After Christ has risen, two angels sit at the tomb, one at the foot and one at the head.

FIRST SOLDIER: Out alas, where am I?
So bright the light about nearby
That my heart wholly
From my skin is shaken.
So fiercely frighted by fantasy
Was I never till this day.
For I know not certainly
If I sleep or waken.

They try to get up together.

SECOND SOLDIER: Where art thou fellow soldier?
　　　　　　　　　All about is wondrous clear.
　　　　　　　　　My wits I want, I lose them here.
　　　　　　　　　Such fear there never was.

THIRD SOLDIER:　I cannot move, not far or near,
　　　　　　　　　My vigour fails, my might, my power,
　　　　　　　　　The heart in my body here
　　　　　　　　　Is leapt out of my breast.

They touch each other and try to wake up.

FIRST SOLDIER:　Yes, we are finished, certainly.
　　　　　　　　　For Jesus is risen, so think I,
　　　　　　　　　Out of the sepulchre mightily.
　　　　　　　　　It seems so to my mind.
　　　　　　　　　Like dead here could I lie.
　　　　　　　　　Speak might I not, no, nor spy
　　　　　　　　　Which way he took, truly -
　　　　　　　　　My eyes became so blind.

SECOND SOLDIER: I will creep forth on my knee,
　　　　　　　　　Till past this peril I can be.
　　　　　　　　　For my way I cannot see,
　　　　　　　　　Neither earth nor stone.

THIRD SOLDIER:　It was a wicked time that we
　　　　　　　　　Nailed him on calvary tree.
　　　　　　　　　He said to us in days three
　　　　　　　　　He would rise again.

FIRST SOLDIER:　There is no use delaying so.
　　　　　　　　　To sir Pilate we must go
　　　　　　　　　And tell him our tale, from top to toe
　　　　　　　　　As truly as we durst.
　　　　　　　　　For if the jews knew as well as we
　　　　　　　　　That he were risen in majesty,
　　　　　　　　　Then that mistake of ours would be
　　　　　　　　　Worse even than the first.

They go to Pilate.

SECOND SOLDIER: Hear us, sir Pilate. Sooth to say,
　　　　　　　　　Jesus that was on Friday slain
　　　　　　　　　Through his might is risen again.
　　　　　　　　　This is the third day.
　　　　　　　　　No forces came there him to fetch
　　　　　　　　　But such a sleep he on us set
　　　　　　　　　That all the three of us could do, was let
　　　　　　　　　Him rise and go his way.

PILATE:　　　　　Now by the oath that to Caesar I swore
　　　　　　　　　You sons of dogs
　　　　　　　　　Shall die therefore.

I shall know the truth ere long.
If I find you secretly
Have sold him to his company,
Then are you worthy for to die,
To right what you did wrong.

THIRD SOLDIER: Now by my rank and name of knight
He rose up in the morning light
By virtue of his own might.
I saw it with my eyes.
He rose up, as I say now
And left us lying, I know not how,
Amazed and in a swoon.
We stayed there like stuck swine.

PILATE: You thief, you traitor
I'll find out your treason at last.
You lout, you liar.
Begone and I tell you, go fast.

FIRST SOLDIER: All the time that he his journey took
I dare neither speak nor look,
But for fear I lay and shook
And lay in a deep dream.
He set his foot upon my back.
Every sinew then did crack.
I would not stand another such smack
For all Jerusalem.

PILATE: You whoreson, you hound,
You putrid poisonous cur.
What, you lay dead on the ground,
And let him fly up in the air?

Sir Caiaphas and sir Annas
What say you to their trespass?
I pray you sirs, in this case
Give me some advice.

CAIAPHAS: Now good sir, I you pray,
Listen to me, to what I say.
I give you this counsel, if I may
And you act by it.
Pray them now sir, patiently,
As they love and honour thee
Here as they stand, all three
To keep it quiet.

ANNAS: Sir bishop, I say with full assent,
That to your counsel I must assent.
Though this foolish prophet to hell we sent,
Through his witchcraft he sneaked away.
Therefore let us call our counsel together
And let us conclude the whole matter,
Or else our laws are undone forever.

PILATE: Now in good faith, right woe is me,
                           And so are you as I can see,
                           That he is risen so secretly
                           And from us has escaped.
                           Now I pray you sirs, as you love me,
                           Keep this knowledge privately
                           Till the council meets, and until we
                           Have heard how he escaped.

He gives them money and they go. The women enter, weeping and looking for Jesus.

MARY MAGDALEN:Alas, my life is all mourning.
                           I wander in woe, my hands I wring.
                           My heart in sorrow and sighing
                           Is set and sadly sore.
                           He that I love above all things
                           Alas, is lowly lying,
                           Why am I so long living,
                           To lose, sweet lord, thy love?

MARIA JACOBI: Mighty God omnipotent
                           Give them thou hard judgement
                           That to my king such malice meant
                           This must be my thought.

MARIA SALOME: No help now to us is sent
                           Against those devils that did offend.
                           His body still to us is lent.
                           Balm for him have I brought.

MARY MAGDALEN:But sister, of us three which one
                           Can remove the great stone
                           That lieth my sweet lord upon?
                           Move it I never may.

MARIA JACOBI: Sister, it will not need one.
                           It seems to me that he is gone.
                           For on the sepulchre sitteth one
                           And the stone is put away.

They look in the tomb.

FIRST ANGEL: What seek ye women here
                           With weeping and unhappy cheer?
                           Jesus, that to you was dear
                           Is risen, believe you me.

SECOND ANGEL: This is the place, be not afraid,
                           Where Jesus our lord was laid.
                           But he is risen, as he said,
                           And gone to Galilee.

MARIA SALOME: Ah, hurry we fast, for anything,

To tell Peter these tidings.
A blessed word we will him bring
If that the truth this be.

MARY MAGDALEN: I will never leave here truly
Till I find comfort in my misery,
And know where he is, certainly.
Here will I sit and weep.

They go. [Mary Magdalen stays] Christ enters wearing a robe, and with a cross-staff in his hand.

JESUS: Why weep thou, woman? Tell me why.
Whom seekest thou so tenderly?

MARY MAGDALEN: My lord, sir, was buried nearby,
And now he is away.
If thou hast done all this annoy
Tell me, sweet sir, hastily,
Right soon this very day.

JESUS: Woman, is not thy name Mary?

MARY MAGDALEN: Ah Lord, I ask thy mercy.

JESUS: Mary, touch not my body
I have not yet been with my father almighty.
But to my brethren go thou, hurry,
And of this see thou certify -
Tell them what thou hast seen.

Mary goes to meet the other women [on their way to where the disciples are].

MARY MAGDALEN: Oh women, now no woe there is.
I spoke with my lord, a little before this.
All that's bad is turned to bliss
I saw him with my eyes.

MARIA JACOBI: Sisters, search we into this
Mirth in mind is not amiss
He said to all whose hearts were his
That to heaven he would fly.

[Mary Salome and Mary Jacobi] go to where Jesus is. [Mary Magdalen goes on to meet Peter]

JESUS: All hail women, all hail.

MARIA SALOME: Ah Lord, we believe thee without fail.
Thou art risen us to heal,
And took us all from woe.

JESUS: Be not afraid, women, of me.
To my brethren now go ye,

And bid them come to Galilee,
To meet me, everyone.

MARY JACOBI: Anon lord, done it shall be.
It will be good that sight to see,
For mankind, lord, is bought by thee,
Through thy great passion.

Mary Magdalen goes to Peter.

MARY MAGDALEN: Peter, tidings good and true.
We have seen my lord Jesu.

PETER: Yea, well are you that have been true.
I foreswore him that I knew.
I am ashamed with him to meet.

Yet I hope to see his face
Though I have done great trespass.
Knowledge of my woe he has,
Of that he may take heed.

Jesus goes over to Peter.

JESUS: Peter knows thou not me?

PETER: Ah Lord, mercy I ask of thee
With full heart, kneeling on my knee.
Forgive me my trespass.
My faint flesh and my frailty
Made me lord, false to thee,
But forgiveness with heart free
Grant me, through thy grace.

JESUS: Think on thine own deed today.
Flesh is frail, and failing aye.
And merciful be thou alway,
As now I am to thee.

Since thou thyself fallen has,
Be more inclined to grant grace.
Go forth. Forgiven is thy trespass.
My blessing be on thee.

GOBBET: Then from West Cheshire, with full good grace,
Our actors will show us Emmaus,
Where Christ appeared to Cleophas.
A fair pageant will you see.

PLAY 16
The Ascension

CAST: Luke
             Cleophas
             Jesus
             Andrew
             Peter [here, last speech shared with Gobbet]
             Thomas
             Two Angels

LUKE: Alas, all well is now away.
             My own, my master, mourn I may.
             Logged he lies beneath the clay.
             My heart is filled with dread.

CLEOPHAS: Brother, gone are days three
             Since he was nailed up on the tree.
             Know thou if he risen be,
             As he before had said?

LUKE: Dear brother Cleophas,
             That would be a curious case.
             Through the heart he wounded was.
             How should he live again?

CLEOPHAS: If he godhead in him has,
             And comes to save man from trespass,
             He may rise through his own grace
             However he be slain.

LUKE: A misty thing it is to me.
             How can I believe such things should be.
             How should he rise in days three?
             Of such wonders none heard say.

CLEOPHAS: Thou sayest true, that well I see.
             My mind cannot teach belief to me.
             But I know God in his majesty
             Can do whatever he may.

Jesus enters dressed as a pilgrim and speaks to them

JESUS: Good men, if your will it were,
             Let me in good manner
             Share in your talking. I would hear
             Of your woe, if I could.

CLEOPHAS: Ah sir, it seems to us here
That thou art a pilgrim. So you appear.
Tidings and tales from everywhere
You may hear as they are told.

In Jerusalem the other day
Thou, that walkest many a way -
May thou not hear what men do say,
As thou this life doth lead?

JESUS: What say thee? Tell me, pray.

LUKE: Of Jesus of Nazareth, in good faith,
A prophet to point all men the way,
And wise in word and deed.
Wise to God and man was he.
But the bishops - accursed may they be -
Damned him and nailed him on a tree,
And wrong he never wrought.

CLEOPHAS: In truth, before believed we
That Israel he would make free,
And out of their pain in majesty
His people would be brought.

LUKE: Yes sir, now is the third day
Since they made this affray.
Some women went to where he lay
Early in the morn.
They frightened us, in faith.
They told us he was stolen away,
And angels, so they say,
Sat the sepulchre before.

CLEOPHAS: Yes sir, these women, as heard I,
Said he had risen readily,
And some men of our company
There at once did go.
They found it so, in less and more.
Our hearts will be full sore
If it be not so.

JESUS: Ah fools, all feeble in your faith.
Learn to believe in God's law.
The prophets before you used to say -
Believe it truthfully -
That it was needful, sooth to say
That Christ should suffer death that day.
To thejoy that will last always
He brings man, in his mercy.

The prophet Esau sayeth this -
'As a woman comforteth
Her child that has done amiss
To make it well, believe ye me,

So God to man is reconciled,
Through his mercy in manner mild.'
And in Jerusalem, from wicked wiles
Redeemed they should be.

CLEOPHAS: Ah lord, give thee good grace
For greatly comforted me thou has.
Go with us to this place.
An inn lies here nearby.

JESUS: Now, good men, sooth to say
I have to go a great way.
So at this time I must say nay.
But I thank you heartily.

LUKE: Sir you shall in the best manner
Stay with us at our supper,
For night is now approaching near.
Stay here, for anything.

Jesus goes with them to the inn

CLEOPHAS: Sit down sir, I you pray
And take a morsel if you may,
For you have walked a great way,
Since today at noon.

JESUS: Thanks to you, good men, in good faith.
I will bless this bread in righteous way.
Listen good men to what I say.
Remember what is done.

He breaks the bread

Eat on men, do it gladly,
In the name of God almighty.
For this bread blessed have I
I give it you today.

Jesus vanishes

LUKE: Thanks sir, certainly
Now I see you be right merry.
What? Where is he that sat us by?
Alas, he has gone away.

CLEOPHAS: Alas alas alas alas.
This was Jesus in this place.
When he broke the bread I knew his face,
But nothing I knew before.

LUKE: A burning heart in us he made.
While he here with us two was
To know him we had not the grace,
For all we heard and saw.

CLEOPHAS: Go we brother, and that anon,
And tell our brethren everyone
How our master is from us gone.
This truly we may say.

LUKE: Yes, well indeed may we make moan.
We sat with him and feasted on,
And no way have him known –
Not till he passed away.

They go to where the other disciples are gathered

CLEOPHAS: Rest well brethren, one and all.
Wonders have to us befall.
Our lord and we were in a hall
Yet saw we not that it was he.

ANDREW: Believe thou well this, Cleophas,
That he is risen that dead was
And to Peter appeared he has
This day, openly.

LUKE: Yet our minds were both in darkness knit
Till the bread was broken into bits.
And then when he had broken it,
He vanished before we knew.

PETER: Now we brothers are all together,
I say we hide us somewhere here,
So the Jews can do us no manner
Of malice, believe you me.

ANDREW: Stay we longer in this place.
It may be God will show us grace
To see lord Jesus face to face
And comforted to be.

All go inside and Jesus stands in the midst of them

JESUS: Peace among you, brethren fair.
Yes, dread you nothing, in no manner.
I am Jesus, do not fear,
That died on calvary.

PETER: Ah what is he that comes here,
To this fellowship altogether
And so to us appears?
A ghost I think I see.

JESUS: Brethren, why be afraid for nought,
Injured at heart by feeble thought?
I am he that bliss has brought
I died for man's good.

My feet, my hands you may see.

To know the truth is granted ye.
In truth I tell you I am he,
He that died upon a tree.

Handle me now, all and one
And believe this everyone.
A ghost has neither flesh nor bone
As you see now on me.

ANDREW: Ah Lord, much joy to us is come.
               But what he is I know none.

JESUS: Since you believe I am no man
               More signs you shall see.

               Have you any meat here?

PETER: Yea, my lord, loved and dear.
               Roasted fish and honey here
               Is all we have for you.

JESUS: Eat we then, in good manner.
               Know me by this supper.
               A ghost to eat has no power,
               As you shall see me do.

Jesus eats, and gives some to his disciples

JESUS: Brethren, I told you before
               When I was with you less than an hour
               That my word, both less and more
               Fulfilled must be.

               For this was written in prophecy.
               I suffer death by necessity,
               And the third day with victory
               Rise to glorious day.

Jesus vanishes. The disciples go to Bethany, where Peter meets Thomas

PETER: Ah Thomas, tidings good and new.
               We have seen the lord Jesu.

THOMAS: I shall never believe that this is true,
               By God omnipotent,
               Unless I see in his hands two
               Holes where the nails go -
               And put my fingers also
               There where the nails went.

ANDREW: Thomas, go we all together.
               Better our enemies to fear
               Than that the Jews should be a danger
               To our fraternity.

THOMAS: Wherever you go, brethren dear
                 I will go with you in good manner.
                 But the tale you tell me here
                 I believe not till I see.

PETER: Now Thomas if thou stay
                 To see him then perhaps thou may
                 And touch him also, in good faith
                 As we have done before.

THOMAS: Wherever you be, there am I, always.
                 But to make me believe these things you say
                 You waste your pains. So I pray
                 Speak of that no more.

They go into the house and lie down. Suddenly Jesus appears

JESUS: Peace my brothers, both one and all.
                 Come hither Thomas, to thee I call.
                 Come forth, whatever may befall.
                 Show thy hand and put it here.
                 See my hands and see my feet,
                 Put in thy hand. Don't hesitate.
                 My wounds are still fresh, still wet
                 As they first were.

                 And be though no more so dreading
                 But ever true believing.

Thomas puts his hand in the wounds in Christ's side

THOMAS: My God, my lord, my Christ, my king.
                 Now I believe without doubting.

JESUS: Yes Thomas, thou seest now in me.
                 Now thou believe that I am he.
                 But blessed must they all be
                 That believe and never see

                 Whoever will to this consent –
                 That I am God omnipotent –
                 With you that all be present,
                 My darlings will be, always.

                 Whoever to it will not consent,
                 On the day of judgement
                 In hell fire shall they be burnt,
                 And ever know sorrow and pain.

                 Whoever of my father has any mind
                 Or of my mother, in any kind
                 In heaven bliss they all shall find,
                 Without pain or any woe.

                 You shall, my brothers, through my behest
                 Take virtue of the Holy Ghost.
                 He shall be sent to help you most

When you to the world I send.
My witnesses you all shall be
In Jerusalem and Judee
Samaria also, and each country
To the worlds end.

This thing you shall well know.
Whoever believes steadfastly in you
Such signs in truth shall they show
In marvels and strange tongues also.
Such grace shall be in their doing.
Now to my father am I going.
You, my brothers, take my blessing,
For to heaven I must go.

Jesus ascends

JESUS: My sweet brethren, loved and dear
To me is granted full power
In heaven and earth, far and near
For my godhead in might is most.
To teach all men now go ye
That my word fulfilled will be
In the name of the father and of me
And of the Holy Ghost.

FIRST ANGEL: Who is this that comes within.
To the bliss of heaven he enters in
Bloody out of the world of sin.
Harrowed Hell hath he.

SECOND ANGEL: Comely he is in his clothing
And with full power going,
A number of saints with him leading
Great he seems in majesty.

Jesus pauses

JESUS: I that spoke of righteousness
I that brought men from distress -
Redeemer is my name, and so I was,
Of all mankind, through grace.
My people were from me beguiled
Through sin and through the devil's wiles.
To heaven I bring them,
All that in hell were.

THIRD ANGEL: Why is thy clothing now so red,
Thy body bloody, and thy head?
On thy clothes the stain has seeped and spread
Like winepress steeped in wine.

JESUS: The devil and his power
That brought mankind in danger
Through death on a cross and blood so clear
All have I made mine.

These bloody drops that now ye see
Shall all fresh reserved be
Till I come in my majesty
To doom the last day.
This blood I shed - witness to me -
I died for man on the rood-tree.
I rose again within days three.
With such love I loved thee.

These drops now with good intent
To my father I will present
That good men shall have testament
And know me openly.
Graciously their bliss I bought.
The wicked also shall be taught
How worthily their doom is wrought
When I return that day.

He ascends. The angels sing. Angels descend

FIRST ANGEL: You men that be of Galilee
Whereupon now wonder ye
Waiting for him that in majesty
Now went from you?

SECOND ANGEL: Jesus Christ, believe you me,
Who went to heaven, as you see,
Right so come again will he
As you saw him go.

PETER: Hear brothers what these angels say,
That Jesus through his might and main
To heaven is gone and will come again
Just as forth he went.

JOHN: Now must we start believing
For both by sight and touching
Speaking, eating and drinking
He proves his deity.

ANDREW: Yea, also by his upraising
Seems he fully heaven's king.
He who lives believing
Saved life and soul is he.

PETER: Go we brothers, with one assent
And fulfill his commandment.
Beware that fear may force dissent
Believe all steadfastly.

[GOBBET]   Pray we all with full intent.
That his spirit unto us be sent.
Jesu, that from us now went,
Save all this company.

PLAY 17

Interlude

CAST: **Gobbet**
                   Jesus
                   God

GOBBET: Now our Lord from us is gone
                   Of comfort here we may have none –
                   Only his word, to put our trust upon.
                   We have him no more in sight.
                   Let us be strong then in our prayers.
                   For well I know, from him I learned,
                   That he will send a counsellor,
                   Down from the heavenly light.

                   Come Holy Ghost, come creator.
                   Visit our thoughts in time of care.
                   Thou art man's conqueror.
                   Grant us, lord, thy grace.

Christ speaks in heaven

CHRIST: Glorious father, fair and free,
                   You know in the wisdom of your deity
                   That I have done your will.
                   The apostles that you called to me
                   Want wisdom, grace, prosperity.
                   May your word to them be fulfilled.

GOD: My son, beloved, kind and dear,
                   What you ask is always heeded here,
                   Health and faith is in your prayer.
                   I know your clear intent.
                   In will full liberal and clear,
                   My spirit will to them appear
                   To make them wiser than they were.
                   That has my full assent.

                   The Holy Ghost to earth goes down,
                   With seven gifts of full renown,
                   Theirs to have, through devotion.
                   He will confirm them, though they be sad,
                   That they in time may all be bound
                   In heaven's bliss to wear the crown,
                   Ever to reign in its possession,
                   Thereto be mery and glad.

                   No dread of death, and no distress,

Will shake them from their steadfastness.
Such love in them, such goodness,
My spirit will ever inspire.
Steadfastness in them is there none,
But when my spirit is them upon,
They shall be as stiff as stone,
Through force of heavenly fire.

God sends his holy spirit

GOBBET: Ah, mercy, Lord, full of grace.
I feel and see thee in this place.
I am wiser than I was.
Thou makest my heart full light.

My belief is now so clear
And love in my heart is printed so fair,
That no man, in no manner,
To move my mind has might.

I believe in God omnipotent,
That made heaven and earth and firmament,
With steadfast heart and true intent,
And he is my comfort.

I believe - this is my testament -
In Jesus, his son, from heaven sent,
True Christ, that saved all earthly men,
And is our elders' lord.

And I believe and truth can tell,
That he in spirit went to Hell,
Delivered all those that there did dwell,
And rose the third day.

And I believe fully this,
That he went up to heaven bliss,
And on his father's right hand is,
To reign for ever and aye.

And I believe with heart steadfast,
That he will come at the last
And doom mankind for actions past
The living and the dead.

And my belief shall be at the most,
By virtue of the Holy Ghost.
And through his help, without a boast,
My life I mean to lead.

PLAY 18
The Judgement

CAST:

God
Two Angels
Jesus
Four of the saved
Satan
Devils
Two of the damned
Matthew
Mark
Luke
John

GOD:

Ego sum alpha et omega, primus et novissimus.

I, God, greatest of degree,
In whom no beginning or end may be,
I that am peerless in potency,
Openly now appear.
In my godhead are persons three.
Mine is the power that none may flee.
The sovereignty that is in me
Shall always shine out clear.

For your sins I come on high,
To make a reckoning of the right.
Now to the doom I wield my might
That the dead all duly dread.
Therefore, my angels fair and bright,
Awake the world to look on light
That I may see all in my sight
That I for them may bleed.

Show you my cross, display it clear,
The crown of thorns, the sponge, the spear,
The nails - show them to those that lived in fear
Of when they would see this day.
Show the garment that I wear,
That marks of all my wounds doth bear.
The stoutest at this sight shall stare
Standing in street or sty.

FIRST ANGEL:

Lord, that madest through thy might,
Heaven and earth, day and night,
All distance falls before our flight
When we your bidding do.
To awake the world to look on light,
I shall be ready, here on high,

They shall be shown all in your sight,
Thou shall see them, Lord, full soon.

SECOND ANGEL: Take our trumpets fast, a blast to blow,
All mankind shall know.
If man a good account can show
Soon it shall be seen.
They that did well in their living
They shall have joy without ending.
They that were bad, without mending,
Shall ever have sorrow and grief.

The angels take up their trumpets and blow. All the dead rise from their graves.

JESUS: You good and evil in this place,
Come to the judgement of righteousness.
The deeds of love I did thee, more and less,
I will tell again here.
On earth through me made man thou was,
Put in a place of great cleanness,
From which in thy wickedness
Cast away thou were.

When thou had done this trespass
I waited, for which the best way was,
To recover thee in this case
Into my company.
How could I do thee more grace
Than take the same form thou hast?
Here now in this place
That is shown openly.

I died on the rood-tree.
My blood was shed, as you can see,
To deprive the devil of his potency,
To win back what you threw away.
That blood - behold thee -
Fresh till now I wished to be,
That to my father almighty
I might offer it on this day.

My blood now shown is
That the good might have bliss -
They that avoided wickedness,
And ever good works wrought.
The evil also, that did amiss,
Must have great sorrow in sight of this.
They have lost the joy that should be his
Whom Christ on rood-tree bought.

Now you shall openly see
Your saviour bleed, man, for thee.
The good to joy go, blessedly,
The evil to damnation.
Behold now, all men. Look on me,
See my fresh blood flee,

That I bled on the rood-tree,
For your salvation.

Blood flows from his side.

How dare you ever do amiss
Had you but thought of this -
I bled to bring you all to bliss
I suffered so much woe.
I come to you in righteousness.
Look into yourselves. I tell you this -
Each must reckon the sins that are his.
That is just and must be so.

ONE OF THE SAVED:
Lord receive me to thy grace.
Pain have I suffered in this place.
Although I foul and wicked was
Washed is it all away.

SECOND OF THE SAVED:
And I lord, on thee cry and call,
Thy own Christian, and thy thrall,
That of my sins am purged, of all,
For thy joy I pray.

JESUS:
Come here to me, my darlings dear,
That blessed in the world always were.
Take my realm, all together,
Ordained for you it was.
While I was on earth here,
You gave me meat, in good manner,
So in the light of heaven clear
You shall ever dwell for this.

In my thirst you gave me drink.
Naked, you gave me clothing.
When I needed safe harbouring,
You harboured me from cold.
Other deeds to my liking
You did on earth while you were living.
Your reward in heaven for each thing
Will be a thousandfold.

THIRD SAVED:
Lord, I do not understand.
When I lived above the ground.
Thee in misery could I never find
To show you my good will.

FOURTH SAVED:
No, certainly. I cannot bring to mind,
That ever to thee I was so kind.
Thee could I never find
Such kindness to fulfill.

JESUS: Yes, forsooth, my friends dear.
                   Any who poor and naked were
                   You clad and fed them, both together,
                   And harboured them also.
                   Such as were in great danger
                   In prison on the earth here,
                   You visited them, in a humble manner,
                   You helped them in their woe.

                   Therefore, my angels, go you anon,
                   Divide my chosen, every one,
                   From those that have been my foes
                   And bring them into bliss.
                   They shall sit on my right hand,
                   For so I gave them to understand
                   When they did, in heart and hand,
                   My bidding not amiss.

FIRST ANGEL: We will never cease, once we begin
                   Till they are brought to bliss within,
                   The souls without a stain of sin,
                   Full soon, as you shall see.

SECOND ANGEL: I know them well, that task is mine,
                   The bodies, lord, that be thine.
                   Joy shall they have, without a pain,
                   That never shall ended be.

The angels sing. All the saved follow them.   [Satan and] Devils enter.

SATAN: Ah righteous judge, and lord of light,
                   That there are sat to judge the right,
                   Mercy thou hast, if thou might,
                   To save these men from pain.
                   But let me have what is my right.
                   Those that are sinful in your sight
                   I reckoned their up deeds.
                   I can prove these men are mine.

                   Judge this man mine, here in this place.
                   He deserves it, for his trespass.
                   He ought to be thine, thou hast the grace,
                   But in sin he became all mine.
                   A Christian man I know he was,
                   Knew good from evil in each case,
                   But my commandment done he has,
                   And ever forsaken thine.

                   Through mercy all these might be thine,
                   They're mine through wickedness and sin,
                   Thine through the passion you put yourself in,
                   And mine by my temptation.
                   To me obedient they were, always.
                   Thy commandment they cast away.
                   Thou righteous judge, therefore I pray,
                   Doom them to my prison.

These here, they would never know
Poor men, or charity to them show.
So, drive them all from you,
Now they stand before your face,
I shall lead them a dance down low.
Where fire shall burn though no man blow.
I'll have them tied up in a row.
They can never pass out of that place.

FIRST DEVIL: Nay, I will dispute with him on this.
You sit as high justice.
If you be righteous
Hand them over to me.
These words God said, no less,
And Matthew bears witness,
A man is judged by what his deed was -
Can you answer to that - lets see.

SATAN: You said in your testament
That when you came to judgement
The angels from thee would be sent
To part the evil from the good,
And put them into torment,
With weeping and groaning fervent
Which words - to all you scholars present -
I will now rehearse -

'Sic erit consummatione seculi: exibunt angeli et seperabunt malos de medio justorum, et mittent eos in caminum ignis, ubi erit fletus et stridor dentium'.

So.   Deliver to me these men,
And by my prick and by my pen
I'll make them grin.
I'll make them cry.
In as hot a chimney
As ever you made for me
Baked they'll be,
They'll burn, they'll fry.

JESUS: Lo, you men that wicked have been,   *242*
What Satan says, you hear and see.
A righteous doom you cannot flee.
My grace I put away.
When the time of grace was lasting
To seek it you had no liking.
So I must, for everything,
Give righteous doom today.

When I was hungry and thirsty both,
And naked, you would not give me clothes.
Sick, and in great woe,
You would not visit me,
Nor yet in prison to me come,
Nor of your meat to give me some,

Nor harbour me within your home,
It was never your will to me.

FIRST DAMNED: When wast thou naked or homeless,
Hungry, thirsty or in sickness,
Or in any prison-house?
We never saw thee cold.

SECOND DAMNED: But if we had thee hungry or thirsty seen,
Naked, sick or in prison been,
Homeless, or in any need,
Then certainly we would.

JESUS: Nay, when you saw the least of mine,
That on earth suffered pain,
You would offer nought of thine,
To answer my desire.
And since you would nothing incline
To help those poor of mine,
Your love to me, it was not fine.
So go ye to the fire.

SATAN: Ah Lord judge, my thanks to thee.
Go we to Hell all hastily.
For you have lost - right as did I -
The bliss that lasts forever.
You're sent down to my belly
Where endless pain is, and misery.
One thing I tell you truly -
You'll be delivered - never.

The devils carry them off. The four evangelists enter.

MATTHEW: I, Matthew of this bear witness.
For in my gospel my words express
All that my Lord of his goodness
Has rehearsed here.
By me all men were warned before
To save their souls evermore.
Now, through misliking, they are forlorn,
And damned to fire in fear.

MARK: I, Mark, to you directly say
That they were warned in many a way,
In their living never to go astray
If heavens bliss they would recover.
Excuse themselves they never may.
They deserved it, in good faith -
To suffer the judgement given today,
To be damned forever.

LUKE: And I Luke, on earth living,
Wrote of my Lord's work in everything,
And taught it, in all my cunning,

That every man might know.
So I say in this -
No excuse there is.
Against my words they did amiss,
They must suffer so.

JOHN: And I, John the evangelist,
               Bear witness too to this.
               In me they might have put their trust
               And not have done amiss.
               All that my Lord said here
               I wrote it in my manner.
               All that you need to know is here.
               Put all your trust in this.

Epilogue

JESUS: Before we go, print these sayings on your mind and heart.
Record them and keep them in memory.
Continue in my word, do not from it depart.
Then shall all men know most perfectly
That you are my disciples and my family.
Do nought without me, let my word be your guide.
Then in your doings you shall always well speed.
For, I am the son of God, the light of this world.
He that follows me walks not in darkness.
He has the light of life, as the scriptures record.
Patriarchs and prophets have told you of this.
Abraham, Isaac and Jacob to my coming bear witness.
To them I was promised before the world began,
To pay their ransom, to become a man.
If you love me heartily
And keep my bidding truly
To my father pray will I
To send his holy ghost.
For we are the holy trinity.
So it was in the beginning, I say to thee.
So it is, so will it always be.
Amen.